Jaime Cisterna

BETWEEN FEAR AND FAITH

Endorsement by
Franklin Graham

Between FEAR and FAITH
Finding the Courage to Not Waste Your Life

© Jaime Cisterna

ISBN 978-1-7380456-0-0

First Edition in Portuguese, *Entre o Medo e a Fé*, 2020

First Edition in English, 2023

Translation from Portuguese: Tiago Cisterna

Editing: Jason Orr, Geoffrey Hale

Cover: Benjamim César

To my dear wife Luisa, and our children Tiago, Débora, Joshua, and Lucas, trusting in God that they may fulfill His mission. I pray that they may not waste their lives wandering in circles, but instead seize the Promised Land.

Acknowledgements

I thank my son Tiago for his dedication in translating this book from the original in Portuguese into English, continuing a project that started around the table at a Sunday lunch, with the support of my wife Luisa, Débora and Lucas.

A special note of thanks goes to the Reverend Franklin Graham who, with surprising readiness, penned his gracious words endorsing this work.

I thank my dear former Criminal Law Professor Guerra, who I have always admired, for his sincere and valuable motivation during the critical writing process.

I also thank my friends Jason Orr and Geoffrey Hale, who were willing to review the final English draft to ensure the book's quality.

In John Bunyan's classic book, "The Pilgrim's Progress", the characters Christian and Hopeful deviate from Pilgrim's Way to rest in Doubting Castle, in which lived a great and terrible giant named Despair. Upon finding them, the giant drags them to a dungeon and puts them in chains. He flogs them and leaves them to rot in a cell, only feeding them bread and water. Starving, injured, and severely discouraged, Christian and Hopeful even consider ending their own lives. They both remain locked in that dungeon for many days, until they realized something crucial: the key that Christian carried in his chest pocket could open any door—the key called Promise! "What a fool I have been, to lie like this in a stinking dungeon, when I could have just as well walked free. In my chest pocket I have a key called Promise that will, I am thoroughly persuaded, open any lock in Doubting Castle." And so, the two pilgrims stood up, opened the door to their cell, and left, returning to the King's Highway.

Contents

Endorsement by Franklin Graham

My friend Jaime Cisterna, who served as my interpreter in Rio de Janeiro, Brazil, has turned a bright light on a fascinating passage of Scripture focusing on the Hebrew spies who went into the Promised Land. Instead of entering by faith in the Lord, the majority allowed fear to seize their hearts, missing the blessings God had for them. Jaime points out that "going against the majority requires great courage." Readers will be thrilled to see what happens when people find themselves "Between Fear and Faith," choosing to be courageous because of the promises of God.

Franklin Graham, President and CEO
Billy Graham Evangelistic Association
Samaritan's Purse

Testimonial by José Guerra

Between FEAR and FAITH, I met the author of this remarkable work of literature. I was a professor of Criminal Law and Prosecutor of the First Jury Court in the city of São Paulo, Brazil. Jaime Cisterna was one of my students. He was brilliant, intelligent, even-minded, creative, and sensible. His appearance (I remember well!) had the markings of a future judge. When he graduated from Law School in 1991, the world of law in Brazil was still celebrating the recently enacted Brazilian Federal Constitution, pouring over the studies pertinent to the new juridical order by it imposed.

Excitingly, now my former student treats us with his necessary reflection on fear and faith. For me, this is a grand and splendid reunion! I have read everything with layman's eyes. I believe the magnificence of the themes written here deserve deep reflection. They spoke to my deepest fear, regulated by a faith oftentimes awoken by that very same fear.

Indeed, it may be better to warn against fear without faith, for do we not know that it breeds hatred, anger, and violence? Or what about fleeing, which deceitfully comforts our soul in a way alien to the divine will? Or bring up a certain aversion to suffering, built either by flight itself, or by despair, which currently so contaminates us? Or even still, to think of those who have not yet died, but remain barely alive; those whose only lingering perspective on life is that of hopelessness? Or, finally, picture the terrible fate of those who suffer through innumerable traumas and end up losing life without dying?

Undoubtedly, it is faith in God that overcomes, relieves, restores, strengthens, encourages, and moves. And despite intermittent turbulence, it is the path that brings protection and aid, building a peace that results in the true understanding of God's divine nature.

The themes of this book are complex and thought provoking. I confess that it led me through a deep dive into my own existence and into a whirlwind of emotions. I know that fear, to a certain extent, keeps us from many evils, but I also need to better understand that it is faith in God that will always lead to and be the ultimate cause of true happiness and wellbeing for all mankind.

Hence the importance of carefully reading this work by Jaime Cisterna, to whom I am grateful for the happy reunion this book has provided me.

José Guerra Armede
Professor of Criminal Law (retd), and former Prosecutor of the First Jury Court in São Paulo, Brazil

Foreword by Geoffrey Hale

Ancient Egypt is a long way from 21st century North America. However, many Christians – and others who look at the effects of social disruption on many contemporary churches – can benefit from Jaime Cisterna's study of faith and fear in the Book of Numbers. *Between Fear and Faith* explores the biblical narrative of Israel's critical decision to reject God's calling to enter the Promised Land in Numbers 13-14, the consequences of their giving into fear rather than trusting in God's visible presence and promises, and the implications of these long-ago events for Christians today.

The Exodus from Egypt is both the historical narrative of Israel's deliverance from slavery and a symbol of divine deliverance rooted in God's purpose to guide His people to the Promised Land, fulfilling His ancient promise to Abraham. It also demonstrates the critical importance – and our frequent misunderstanding of – faith as a necessary condition of entering the promises and potential which God offers to those who trust in Him.

Pastor Cisterna draws a clear distinction between generic and biblical concepts of faith. "Generic" faith reflects of aspiration towards or hope in "the full range of possibilities life has to offer", whatever the challenges or difficulties which may stand in the way of achieving these hopes. The biblical principle of faith in God responds to His direct revelation of Himself, as in the Exodus narrative, and to the authoritative revelation in Scripture of His past dealings with, purposes for, and promises to humankind. Growing (or mature) faith reflects a trust in God's revelation of His nature, character, care for and promises to His people. Pastor Cisterna contrasts these conditions with what he calls "faith in fear" – a reaction against vulnerability to an indifferent or hostile world resulting in efforts to take control of our own lives and destiny in ways that disregard God or push Him to the margins of our lives and priorities.

New Testament writers clearly indicate that God's revelation of Himself in the Hebrew Bible, the Christian "Old Testament," are meant for the example for all those who claim to follow Christ. These stories contrast God's self-revelation with against distorted understandings of God that contribute to a heartening of hearts towards Him and the "idolatry" that so often accompanies these things amid the challenges and sufferings of a fallen world.

Pastor Cisterna demonstrates the relevance of the ancient story of Israel's turning away from the Promised Land in Numbers 14 to the realities of the modern human condition. Better by far the pathways of genuine faith as a living, growing trust for a God who is infinitely greater than His creation and faithful to His promises to those who trust in Him – whatever the challenges of our lives.

Geoffrey Hale, M.Div., Ph.D.

Introduction:
Because I live, you also will live.

To be commanded to love God at all, let alone in the wilderness, is like being commanded to be well when we are sick, to sing for joy when we are dying of thirst, to run when our legs are broken. But this is the first and great commandment, nonetheless. Even in the wilderness - especially in the wilderness - you shall love him.
Frederick Buechner

Faith is to believe what you do not yet see; the reward for this faith is to see what you believe.
Augustine of Hippo

"Have you ever asked yourself how many times you act on faith every day?" was Billy Graham's question in one of his sermons. "The truth is, we live by faith all the time, and without faith it would be impossible to live," he added. While we might think of faith strictly as a strong belief in God or the doctrines that underlie our salvation, the exercise of faith is present in our lives more often than we think, in the big and small decisions we make every day.

As he continued to preach, Rev. Graham spoke of how those people who were listening to him had sat on the seats in that stadium without questioning whether they were safe or not. "Did you inspect the chair before you sat down, or did you send it to a lab first to be tested? No, of course not. You believed it would hold you down, probably because it has happened so many times before, and you've seen it hold others back. too. And yet you acted by faith when you sat in the chair. At the same time, it was unreasonable for you to do that".

Believing, in the sense of sitting in a chair without checking whether it is safe, carries the idea of trusting something or someone. It is like when we get on a plane and trust that the pilot will take us to the desired destination, even though we don't know him or her and have never even seen him or her before. In the same way, we make decisions almost automatically, based only on the circumstances around us, going with the flow, without considering the presence, the promises, and the power of

God at work in our lives. How many things we fail to appreciate in our lives by not trusting Jesus or by not seeing life through the lens of faith in Him.

In 2009, I had the privilege of serving some communities in need in Paraguay along with a team from Samaritan's Purse. Our team offered many services in the medical, optical, and dental fields. As such, we would daily spend hours tending to the hundreds of people who had lined up to our location since early morning.

Particularly, I remember an emotional scene in one of these visits where an elderly man had been given a new pair of eyeglasses by our staff. He immediately erupted in laughter, then soon after, in tears. He rejoiced for finally being able to see, all the while simultaneously mourning for having lived so many years without the ability to appreciate all the beauty around him.

It was as if, at that very moment, a curtain was lifted, and a whole new world now presented itself before him. Still, the joy of having even just a glimpse of this wonderful gift brought with it grief, as he was now acutely aware of all the things that had passed by him unnoticed for so many years.

Behind the tears over his rugged face and his toothless smile, it was possible to visualize a practical lesson regarding our own attitudes. In observing his happiness combined with grief, I thought of how our own hopes and frustrations were also intertwined, as if they were just one emotion. Sometimes we cannot even discern where the pain ends, and joy begins.

In the same way, this also occurs with faith and fear. There are times where our past failures insist on launching a dark cloud of doubt over what should be a bright and confident hope for tomorrow. In fact, these past disappointments can be powerful enough to stop us right in our tracks. Fear, as opposed to faith, produces in us a shocking existential short-sightedness, capable of leading anyone to completely waste their lives.

As time passes, we begin to feel as if life is slowly slipping away from us, like water running through our fingers. It then creates an overwhelming sense of anxiety, leading us to think that each passing day is just another failure or missed opportunity. It builds up, day after day, eventually turning into despair.

It is true that some can see beyond this frustration, into the full range of possibilities life has to offer. For this reason, they seek to make the most out of it. Even so, this may not always be possible, as opportunities might simply never come their way, or they lack freedom to pursue their dreams. What do we do when our faith is faced with injustice or rejection?

Meanwhile, there are those slow to wake up to life. With foggy eyes, they have a hard time seeing through those special lenses, missing the minute details of life—its bright colours and the many attractive or otherwise irresistible features. They live as if parts of their own life had somehow been hidden away or even robbed from them. At the very least, they lack inner strength and perspective in life. Fear is a powerful force that can lead to inertia. Consequently, many people allow fear to keep them trapped in their comfort zone.

I occasionally meet people like this. They have become so frustrated it leaves them wondering if there is anything left in life they would still enjoy doing. They simply prefer to say they are just "surviving", always with an unfortunate and defeated look on their face. Maybe they haven't dove into the realm of God's grace, and thus, never learned to lean on His forgiveness and His desire to lead us into the gift of life found only in His Son, Jesus.

Fundamentally, this divine life must reside within us. If one seeks to live - in the full and exuberant sense of the word - they must understand that they cannot depend on mere circumstances around them. Circumstances come and go, as their causal, unforeseen, or sporadic nature makes them inherently unpredictable. They do not exist on their own, but are instead caused by a host of factors, both good and bad.

This is not the case with our Lord. "Because I live, you also will live" was the promise of the life-giving Savior in John 14:19. It doesn't take much to conclude that such wonderful promise requires faith from those who hear it. Thus, faith is the only way His life comes to us. Further, it is not just the day we trust Him for salvation that we must believe, but every day thereafter we must look to Jesus, "the author and finisher of our faith."

I believe it was Mark Twain who said that courage is resistance to fear, mastery of fear, not absence of fear. The question, however, is where do we find such courage to resist and even overcome our fears? How do we conquer them? While some good advice suggests keeping a good perspective of life in the face of any challenge; or that we should identify our strengths and explore different scenarios of the situation, among other things, nothing - I insist, nothing replaces faith in God. He alone "is our refuge and strength, an ever-present help in trouble. Therefore, we will not fear" (Psalm 46:1-2). Despite difficult circumstances, it takes belief in something bigger to act with courage. This is where faith comes into play.

The heart should not dictate rules as if it were a god, and neither should circumstance. The heart was created to be God's dwelling place, and circumstances, to glorify him.

So, fear must be conquered by faith, but you must believe like a fighter. Be real - no pretense. Roll up your sleeves (i.e.: get down on your knees, open the Word), and fight your thoughts, your doubts, whenever necessary. The fact is, we need to constantly exercise our faith muscles, so they don't atrophy. We learn this from Joshua and Caleb, from the time of their youth in the desert with Moses, to when they became leaders of the nation during the conquest of the Promised Land.

We, too, need to persevere and let our lives be evidence and examples of our faith. Let's feed our souls on God's Word and resist the temptation to give in to the pressures of fear. We must not believe their lies when they are presented to us. Instead, let's pray and deliberately place our trust in God's character, so that the assurance of His love for us will control our minds and hearts.

We are in a delicate position when it comes to our life choices, as so many factors reveal our vulnerabilities. How, then, can we trust ourselves with such complexities? The Bible mentions how deceiving the human heart can be and that we should not trust its desires and intentions. Rather, we should look to God and trust that His will is truly best for us.

Circumstances are passing and fragile, and do not have the strength needed to sustain meaning in life. We should make the best use of them, but they cannot be the rule. Something else is necessary, something bigger and stronger, lest we be washed away by the everchanging trends of each moment, or by the evermoving train of history without making history, least of all our own. Like a rubber band becomes loose after being stretched one too many times, we risk being pulled in every direction, eventually passively accepting any situation.

> *The direction our life takes cannot simply be at the mercy of mere circumstance, nor be determined accidentally by simple reaction.*

Unfortunately, we tend to only value things we can see with our short-sighted vision, often lacking proper insight to observe nuances in things written between the lines. They could be loaded with important messages or meanings and could even be fundamental to properly enjoying life.

Despite our inherent (though limited) desire to enjoy life, lack of faith makes it impossible for eyes to accurately assess the real value of what they see. This is important, as the value we give things often determines how we respond to them. If we view something as precious, we will naturally be attracted to it, loving it, and showing admiration. If we view it as insignificant, however, we may despise it.

The question that naturally arises is how can we be certain that our eyes are in good enough condition to properly determine the true value of something or someone? Only by asking this type of question we can come to the realization that our vision is not the 20/20 we expected. Instead, clearly and accurately seeing all the minute details of life, we need to understand we have an existential short-sightedness, keeping us from correctly valuing things life offers us.

Many times, we come to realize far too late that something we previously saw as insignificant was in fact of great importance. Little by little, our eyes open and we start to see things that previously we could not. Some discover this late in life after unknowingly investing too much in things of little value. For this reason, we need grace in our relationships with others, which itself comes from our relationship with God. This helps us enhance the interpretation and perspective of life and its many characters.

It is surprising how much of life we waste. Despite it being freely given to us, we insist on focusing on its frivolous aspects rather than on life itself. Rui Barbosa, a famous Brazilian writer and diplomat, said he would never substitute faith for superstition, nor reality for an idol.[1] For many others, however, I would argue quite the opposite. We live in a time where a seemingly perfect world is displayed to us through the windows of social media, where every image is carefully edited with all kinds

---

[1] The complete phrase is found in his "Parliamentary Discussions", collected in the pamphlet "Conservative Republican Party". Ministry of Health and Education, Rio de Janeiro, 1897, Tomo I, p. 77

of filters, colors, cuts, and corrections. It is alarming how great an idol these have become. We create façades, mere imitations of an inexistent life, while the real and physical life fades away unnoticed right before our eyes.

I often get the impression that we go through life acting as if we were performers in a play or as characters on a movie screen, merely pretending to live. We are deeply afraid of reality and try our best to escape—a natural response to fear. Faith in fear prefers the comforts of the *status quo*, decisively and aggressively fighting against everything and everyone in hopes of protecting its view of reality; it tries to dominate us and interferes in our every decision. If only we could use the same force of will to destroy it!

To truly face life, it is necessary to dispel this shadow of fear that constantly haunts us. Faith in fear blocks our path, preventing us from fully embracing life and living it to the fullest. We cannot make major life decisions based on fear or according to what people tell us through their limited lenses. It's one thing to be surrounded by dangers and challenges, it's another to decide whether to allow them to limit the way we live. We are surrounded by eyewitnesses of life. Some are driven by constant fear - far beyond careful precaution for survival (what we call instinct), while others prefer to trust God and His promises. Who are we listening to? Often – more than we think, it's their word against His.

Thus, this book is an invitation to trust God. It discusses the biblical story of the *not-conquest* of the Promised Land by the Jewish people as found in the Book of Numbers, chapters 13 and 14. Fear took hold of the people and turned their long-awaited dream into an impossibility: "And why couldn't they go in? Because they didn't trust him" (Hebrews 3:19, TLB). Thank heavens, it was also true that there was a small number among them who had confidence in God amid that environment of fear. It was this smaller group that finally led the people to fulfil their dream many years later, when – "by faith" – even the walls of Jericho fell. (Hebrews 11:30).

Oh, that we may go to Him who never abandons us so that He could teach us to love, to live.

Enjoy the read,

Jaime Cisterna
Calgary, July 2023.

01 Through the Lenses of Fear and Faith

It is not death that a man should fear, but he should fear never beginning to live.
Marcus Aurelius

Every ant knows the formula of its anthill, every bee knows the formula of its beehive. They know it in their own way, not in our way. Only humankind does not know its own formula.
Fiodor Dostoevski

We see either the dust on the window or the view beyond the window, but never the window itself.
Simone Weil

After 430 years of living as slaves in Egypt,[2] God freed the nation of Israel in spectacular fashion. It saw an estimated two million people leave the land of Goshen in northern Egypt,[3] towards Canaan around the year 1446 B.C. We know that it had to be a great multitude, as the number of able-bodied men alone totalled 600,000,[4] not counting women and children.

The whole affair was an extraordinary adventure. It began with the people leaving their homes in Goshen and their miraculous crossing of the Red Sea. Three months later, they arrived at Mt. Sinai, where they received the Tablets of the Law from God.[5] Finally, two years after leaving Egypt, they arrived at the borders of the Promised Land, in Kadesh-Barnea, in the deserts of Paran and Zin.[6]

This land had been promised by the Lord to the nation of Israel through their father Abraham around 600 years earlier. Yet for the past 430 years the people waited for this promise, suffering under the pain of slavery in Egypt. Year after year they had waited, with generations coming and going, never living to see their deliverance. But now, with Moses as their leader, it was finally time for this grand promise to be fulfilled.

---

[2] Exodus 12:41
[3] Genesis 45:10
[4] Exodus 12:37, Numbers 1:45-46
[5] Exodus 19:1; 20:1
[6] Numbers 1:1; 12:16; 20:1

No longer would these people be just another one of the countless generations that had to tell their children of a future deliverance. It would be future generations, this time, who would remember these people as the ones chosen to finally taste the fulfilment of that wonderful promise. Like an Olympic relay race, the baton of hope had been passed one last time, with the expectation that they would finally cross the finish line to receive the coveted prize.

With this historical background in mind, we see that God had fulfilled His word, and that the Promised Land was right in front of them. All that was left was to take the next few steps to cross the border and the rest would be history. Something unprecedented happened instead. After many long years of waiting, then the difficult journey through the desert, Israel became afraid of the tribes already there and backed down.

Chapters 13 and 14 of the Book of Numbers should have been a glorious conclusion to what had been a long and difficult journey, but it instead tells of a melancholic triumph of fear over faith. This unfortunate choice by the Israelites is noted in the Book of Deuteronomy, with words by Moses 40 years later. It explains to the children of that fearful generation the unbelief of their parents:

> Then, as the Lord our God commanded us, we set out from Horeb and went toward the hill country of the Amorites through all that vast and dreadful wilderness that you have seen, and so we reached

> Kadesh Barnea. Then I said to you, "You have reached the hill country of the Amorites, which the Lord our God is giving us. See, the Lord your God has given you the land. Go up and take possession of it as the Lord, the God of your ancestors, told you. Do not be afraid; do not be discouraged."

Moses' joy and enthusiasm in this historic moment was clear and evident: "We have finally arrived! Now go and enter the land." However, the people's reaction was frigid:

> Then all of you came to me and said, "Let us send men ahead to spy out the land for us and bring back a report about the route we are to take and the towns we will come to." The idea seemed good to me; so, I selected twelve of you, one man from each tribe. They left and went up into the hill country and came to the Valley of Eshkol and explored it. Taking with them some of the fruit of the land, they brought it down to us and reported, "It is a good land that the Lord our God is giving us."[7]

I am left wondering what would have happened if history had taken a different path. Firstly, there was no need to have sent those spies like they did, as we will see later; but secondly, even if they still had, it would have been much better if they had returned with a more positive report. Oh, to see the people marching towards their new home filled with enthusiasm, going down in

---

[7] Deuteronomy 1:19-25

history as a generation who trusted the Lord! But, alas, that was not to be. Moses continues in his report by lamenting the many years wasted walking in circles in the desert:

> But you were unwilling to go up; you rebelled against the command of the Lord your God. You grumbled in your tents and said, "The Lord hates us; so, he brought us out of Egypt to deliver us into the hands of the Amorites to destroy us. Where can we go? Our brothers have made our hearts melt in fear. They say, 'The people are stronger and taller than we are; the cities are large, with walls up to the sky. We even saw the Anakites there.'"

The Anakim/Anakites were the descendants of Anak (Genesis 23:2, Joshua 15:13), and occupied the southern lands of Israel, near Hebron. The Israelites were terrified of their stature and compared them to giants: "The people are stronger and taller than we are; the cities are large, with walls up to the sky" (Deuteronomy 1:28, 2:10, 21, 9:2). Despite this, Moses still patiently insisted in their success. He knew the Lord enough to understand that their mission would turn out favorably:

> Then I said to you, "Do not be terrified; do not be afraid of them. The Lord your God, who is going before you, will fight for you, as he did for you in Egypt, before your very eyes, and in the wilderness. There you saw how the Lord your God carried you, as a father carries his son, all the way you went until you reached this place." In spite of this, you did not

trust in the Lord your God, who went ahead of you on your journey, in fire by night and in a cloud by day, to search out places for you to camp and to show you the way you should go.[8]

As Moses reports 38 years later, the Israelites failed to enter the Promised Land because they "did not trust in the Lord". In fact, quite the opposite. They let fear creep in, asking Moses to let them spy the land first before making any attempts to conquer it. God had told them He would give them that land, and that should have been enough.

Our lives are wholly sustained by God, something we usually forget—except in times of crisis. Even then, we constantly search for signs to make us feel safer, ignoring that faith is the greatest sign of all.

But God, rather ironically, concedes and authorizes Moses to let them send the spies on their frivolous mission. Frivolous in the sense that this entire operation was not necessary, and instead simply confirming the

---

[8] Deuteronomy 1:26-33

people's initial hesitation to trust in God's sovereignty. This act of faithlessness on their part was not new, and it could be observed along their entire journey since the very beginning.

One may wonder, then, why God would even allow such an affront to His plans in the first place. It is likely He permitted this to happen precisely to reveal to them their own disbelief. Not only did God clearly promise that He would give them the land of Canaan, He also safely brought them right up to its front door. Their successful journey from Egypt to the gates of Canaan should have been a clear sign of what the following chapters of this story should have been—a simple continuation of God's faithfulness.

But instead of resting on these truths, they chose to distrust God's capability to bring the process to completion. They chose to lean on the words of those spies rather than on the Word of God, which had led them safely thus far. They chose to trust themselves to make this most critical decision, clearly ignoring the invitation to "trust in the Lord with all your heart".[9]

Twelve men, one from each tribe, went out according to the orders given by Moses. For 40 days, they spied upon the land:

---

[9] Proverbs 3:5

> "See what the land is like and whether the people who live there are strong or weak, few or many. What kind of land do they live in? Is it good or bad? What kind of towns do they live in? Are they unwalled or fortified? How is the soil? Is it fertile or poor? Are there trees in it or not? Do your best to bring back some of the fruit of the land."[10]

Along their mission, the twelve spies passed through the desert of Zin until they reached Rehob, where they turned and made their way to the Negeb and soon, Hebron. They then passed along the Valley of Eshkol, where they collected an impressive number of fruits such as grapes, pomegranates, and figs to show the people the bounties of the land God had promised.

One can only imagine the great anticipation of the people as they waited for the spies to return. For 40 days, they waited, probably with great eagerness and many questions. But sadly, once they chose to send those twelve men to spy the land, their path began to deviate from that of God's original plan. The fate of the Israelites now rested on the shoulders of the final report of those men.

We must remember that God had already said that the land was good, so there was no need for their report in the first place. The only thing this would accomplish is create an unnecessary opening for disagreement to

---

[10] Numbers 13:17-20

arise between what the spies would say and what God had already promised. And what could the spies even say? Would they present data that would help the Israelites make a better and more informed decision? Or would it just confirm God's original plan? Or maybe it would let them find the justification they desperately needed to let them return to Egypt—something they had desired from the start?[11]

They preferred to trust the uneventful routine of slavery and the provisions in the desert than to face the unknown and conquer something new God had prepared for them.

Deep down, this incident revealed the true state of Israel's spiritual condition. They thought only of themselves and refused to take part in God's greater plan of redemption. They limited their vision so much, that several times the people voiced their preference for returning to Egypt—to slavery, as long as it gave them some fleeting moment of comfort amidst their fears.

---

[11] Exodus 16:2-3

When the spies finally returned to their camp, their report shocked the people. Using vague and ambiguous language, they described the positives and negatives of what they had experienced, saying that although the land was indeed wonderful, it was sure to present many challenges and dangers. Two of the spies believed that the positives outweighed the negatives, while the other ten saw these challenges as hopeless.

For those ten spies, everything points towards them returning with a verdict already formed, rejecting the divine plan to conquer the land. Though they showed the land's bounties to Moses, they were determined to emphasize the challenges they had discovered:

> We went into the land to which you sent us, and it does flow with milk and honey! Here is its fruit. But the people who live there are powerful, and the cities are fortified and very large. We even saw descendants of Anak there. The Amalekites live in the Negev; the Hittites, Jebusites and Amorites live in the hill country; and the Canaanites live near the sea and along the Jordan.[12]

Canaan, which up until that point was referred to as the *Land Promised by God*[13], then became known as the "Land to which you have sent us." This is a description filled with contempt, cold and negative, that is often

---

[12] Numbers 13:27-29
[13] Numbers 13:2; 14:16, 23, 30, 40; 15.2, etc.

repeated later on. Likewise, a notable lack of words describing the land's bounties also becomes apparent.

Notice the foreboding "but" that stands out in their report as soon as they begin to talk about the obstacles of the land: "But the people who live there are powerful, and its cities are large and fortified." They list off an impressively detailed résumé on the giants who lived there and how great and terrible they were, utterly disregarding the land's positive aspects. As such, this became the alibi they so desperately desired, giving the spies the authority they needed to convince the people that this conquest was simply not possible.

Despite everything quickly going wrong, all was not yet lost. Caleb, one of the twelve spies, then spoke up, aiming to calm the people and convince them of the original plan's viability: "Let us go and take the land. I am sure we will win!"[14] Such enthusiasm, such disposition, such faith in God! This man was different somehow, I am sure of it. He looked at the other leaders and fellow countrymen in the eye, including Moses and the other spies, and resolved to convince everyone that this was the right thing to do.

From the moment Caleb had taken his first glimpse of the new land, especially the beauty of Hebron, which God would give him years later, his eyes were opened. He came to understand what God had planned and

---

[14] Numbers 13:30

would not let anything or anyone get in his way of achieving this dream. He had seen the same fortified cities as the rest, but he did not fear—he had his eyes fixed on the prize. Caleb saw the terror in the people's eyes. He saw they were headed away from God's plans, and he knew he had to intervene.

Going against the majority requires great courage. Faith opens our eyes and allows us to see things that until that point were invisible. This revelation then brings us courage.

Caleb's eyes of faith would never close. We see this same vigor and enthusiasm in him 45 years later when the now 85-year-old would say to Joshua, the new leader: "I am still as strong today as the day Moses sent me out."[15] We will discuss the Israelites eventual return to the Promised Land later on, but even here, Caleb's voice is one of confidence and of one who insists on trusting in the Lord even in the most difficult of circumstances.

However, despite all his efforts, his enthusiasm was not enough to convince the people or his peers. Not for

---

[15] Joshua 14:11

lack of excitement or insufficient passion, but because their hearts were set on something different, something far away from God's plans.

It is difficult to lift someone's spirits when they themselves do not want to be cheered up.[16] The people did not want to hear a single word of encouragement from Caleb but were instead ready for the seeds of discord and division. The other spies' response to Caleb's words were persistent: "We can't attack those people; they are stronger than we are."[17]

With the convincing evidence mounting, the people let themselves be persuaded by the other spies. Their use of exaggerated and passionate language, typically used to sway the weak, worked once more. In their report, the spies convinced the people that the land would devour them, with the tribes living there being so large and powerful, that they would crush them like bugs.[18] Centuries later, the apostle Paul tells us to take care that no one would fool us with apparently convincing arguments.[19] But in the case of the Israelites, it was already too late.

For the people, who until recently had been slaves in another land and spent the last two years wandering the

---

[16] Proverbs 18:2
[17] Numbers 13:31
[18] Numbers 13:32-33
[19] Colossians 2:4

desert, those arguments presented an impossible obstacle. That wandering nation would stand no chance against the fortified dwellers of the region. So, it is not hard to imagine why, after that intense argument, the crowd panicked. They began shouting in loud voices "and wept aloud all that night".[20] Those many thousands of tents, camped only a short distance away from the land dreamed of by their ancestors, soon became filled with grief and anguish.

The spies who were supposed to simply give precise and impartial information, such that the leaders could decide for themselves, tainted the report with alarming language on top of telling their peers what they should do. The Bible says that "the tongue has the power of life and death,"[21] and, the unfounded words brought back by those spies invaded their hearts and destroyed what little faith in God they had left. Fear took hold of them and placed in them a spirit of disbelief, ruining any remaining possibility of them ever conquering that land.

When fear alerts you to danger, take control of it lest it diminish you.

---

[20] Numbers 14:1
[21] Proverbs 18:21

In addition to the fear in their eyes, the Israelites now saw themselves as mere bugs ready to be stepped on and destroyed by those giants. There was always some danger in that operation, but now, at least in their own minds, things were much worse. Their fear presented them not only with a real danger, but an overwhelming one. Luís de Camões, the 16th century Portuguese poet, wrote: "O, how it is, in perilous times, that fear may grow in the face of men, to be greater than the danger itself."[22]

The people out of whom God wanted to make a great nation transformed themselves into a band of alienated rabble and isolated themselves from His plans. They became disoriented, preferring the executioner to the benefactor, and came to think that the best available option was to return to slavery in Egypt:

> If only we had died in Egypt! Or in this wilderness! Why is the Lord bringing us to this land only to let us fall by the sword? Our wives and children will be taken as plunder. Wouldn't it be better for us to go back to Egypt?[23]

In their eyes, the threat those giants represented to them and their families suddenly became greater than any benefit that Canaan could possibly ever offer. So, in true panic, they became guided by their faith in fear, in contrast to the plan God had for them. Fear also served to

---

[22] Free verse translation of Luís Vaz de Camões, The Lusiad, Book IV, verse 29; Os Lusíadas, Edições Melhoramento, 1962, p. 187.
[23] Numbers 14:2-3

reinforce their old desire to return to Egypt, which had been growing within them for a while. Ironically, though they had left Egypt, they brought Egypt with them in their hearts.

This grumbling at the gates of the Promised Land was not an isolated case in their history, but rather, it shows that it was their norm.[24] This is evident in that the Apostle Paul uses them as an example to alert us against such behaviour.[25] Murmuring and complaining characterized that entire generation, turning it into their trademark. Such inconsistency! Those same people who were finally freed after suffering through hundreds of years of slavery became known throughout history as a people who only whined and complained.

More than any previous generation, those men and women could have had the utmost certainty that the land that flowed with milk and honey could be theirs. Sadly, they did not have the resolve to face the challenges presented, to talk with their leaders or even to pray, entrusting everything to the Lord. Instead, they complained, cowering in the corner, spreading lies and rumors, and gathering followers until they were ready to stage a revolt. Grumbling is clearly condemned in the Scriptures, and it should never be typical behavior for any of God's people.

---

[24] Exodus 15-17; Numbers 11:1-9
[25] 1 Corinthians 10:10

To grumble against God's will is to reject His supreme authority and sovereignty.

The author of the Letter of Jude, traditionally held to be Jesus' brother,[26] links murmuring to the behavior of false teachers, who are only concerned for their own self-interest. In their unhappiness and complaining, they seek their own impure desires, charming others, and leading people astray from the truth of God. Jude states that God will exercise His judgement against such false teachers, as their works are contrary to the Faith (the one that was "once for all entrusted to the holy people of God" – Jude 3), and their words are blasphemous.[27]

The apostle Paul also makes a fervent appeal to Christians to show that their faith is true by avoiding division and all types of grumbling:

> Therefore, my dear friends, as you have always obeyed—not only in my presence, but now much more in my absence—continue to work out your salvation with fear and trembling, for it is God who works in you to will and to act in order to fulfill his good purpose. *Do everything without grumbling or arguing,*

---

[26] Matthew 13:55
[27] Jude 14-16

so that you may become blameless and pure, "children of God without fault in a warped and crooked generation." Then you will shine among them like stars in the sky as you hold firmly to the word of life. And then I will be able to boast on the day of Christ that I did not run or labor in vain.[28]

This picture Paul describes was the same critical condition the people of Israel now found themselves in; that is, the stalemate of whether to go into the Promised Land. The situation from Numbers chapter 14 on seems to have gotten out of Moses' control, and the general confusion caused by this panic began to reach its peak. The murmuring, now in full force, was no longer kept inside the tents, and began spilling out into the public. It came to such a point that even the women and children became an excuse for them not submit to God.

What started out as simple grumbling soon morphed into outright rebellion, with the people blaming God for apparently only bringing them here to die.[29] All they needed now was a new leader to embody all their frustrations and serve as the head of their revolt. No longer they desired Moses' leadership—they needed someone who would spare them the trials this new land offered. So, they began talking amongst themselves to choose someone who would return them to Egypt.[30]

---

[28] Philippians 2:12-16
[29] Numbers 14:3
[30] Numbers 14:4

Naturally, Moses and Aaron, the current leaders of the Israelites, were overcome with fear in the face of such an affront towards God. They could barely believe the commotion happening before their eyes, and the only thing they could realistically do was bow to the crowd. At the same time, they were probably also crying out to the Lord for the sake of the people, just as Moses had done many times before, as they knew God would surely condemn the hostile act of their kinsmen.

In a demonstration of grief and indignation, Caleb and Joshua tore their robes before such a lamentable scene.[31]

Faith-trained eyes can see changes in our mood, feelings, and circumstances. And above all, they know God.

Just like Caleb, Joshua had been sent as a spy to the new land. Although they had seen the same things as the other ten spies during their exploratory mission, their perception of its details was fundamentally different. Joshua and Caleb were sure that the same God that had brought them until that point would certainly finish the

---

[31] Numbers 14:5-6

work He had started and would bless them with the land they had dreamt of for so long.

While the ten other spies had spoken little about Canaan itself, Joshua's speech was instead filled with superlatives, emphasizing the bounties that awaited them on the other side of the border: "The land we passed through and explored is exceedingly good," he declares. The Hebrew word used here, מְאֹד, *mo'ed*, has a certain weight to it, and is used to express something grand and abundant. He saw something in that land that exceeded ordinary expectations, something that made him even more eager to possess it.

Joshua's words reveal the stark contrast between his view of God and that of the other ten. He stressed that they should have confidence in the Lord and in the riches of the land He was providing. He had faith that God was in control of the situation and nothing they were facing was a surprise to Him.

It is likely at some point fear would have crossed the minds of both Caleb and Joshua, a natural response to this great challenge. However, it is made clear through their words that this fear was not enough to overcome them and cause them to solely focus on their hardships. Joshua then stands up and challenges his people to please God and put their faith in Him:

> "The land we passed through and explored is exceedingly good. If the Lord is pleased with us, he

will lead us into that land, a land flowing with milk and honey, and will give it to us. Only do not rebel against the Lord. And do not be afraid of the people of the land, because we will devour them. Their protection is gone, but the Lord is with us. Do not be afraid of them."[32]

Like a friend encouraging another, Joshua appeals to his Israelite brothers to put their faith in the Lord.

Love must be firm. We need to be ready to say or hear difficult things.

Joshua calls for the people to repent from their act of rebellion and turn back to the Lord. He was confident that God would lead them into the land; confident He would not abandon them in this crucial moment. His words reveal the level of spiritual understanding he had regarding the sin the people were committing. His words were not just an invitation for the people to trust in God, but also a warning against their rebellion.

However, his plea had the opposite effect. The people, already poisoned by the other ten spies, ignored the invitation, and with great hostility, attempted to silence both Caleb and Joshua by stoning them to death.

---

[32] Numbers 14:7-9

In their own hearts, the Israelites had already killed the only two people in the whole camp that still desired to continue this wondrous journey of faith. And despite only wishing them well, the two men were only found worthy of the crowd's stones.

This was enough for the Lord to intervene. He revealed His glory in the Congregational Tent and called on Moses to give His final verdict to the people. Seeing this occurring, the rebellious crowd ceased their outward revolt, but it was too little too late—their sentence had already been decided.[33]

The Israelites had been so preoccupied with the challenges of this new land that they no longer could appreciate the benefits they already had. The over-inflated size of the apparent obstacles caused them to even look at slavery in Egypt as better and more attractive than the divine opportunity that had been bestowed upon them. While most of the people saw themselves as mere grasshoppers in a field of giants, Caleb and Joshua saw the giants as nothing more than pieces of bread made to be eaten, through their eyes of faith. It was a simple matter of perspective.

Both sides had seen the same land and had been presented with the same promises and challenges but

---

[33] Numbers 14:10-12

responded with completely different attitudes. They had seen things with different lenses, those of fear and faith.

Between the twelve spies, ten let fear kill their dreams, while the other two, by faith, killed fear.

In challenging the people to trust God, Joshua asserted that the current dwellers of the land had lost their *support*, or *protection*. This is an interesting word which, in Hebrew, also means *shade* or *shadow*. It is something vital for those living in a desert, as beneath the heat of the scorching sun in a desolate landscape, shade means protection. Moses, who lived 80 years in the desert, knew the importance of such a shelter and used the same word when writing Psalm 91:

> Whoever dwells in the shelter of the Most High will rest in the *shadow* of the Almighty. I will say of the Lord, "He is my refuge and my fortress, my God, in whom I trust."[34]

Yes, there were indeed giants in those lands, and no, no one was overlooking such a fact. They were most certainly fierce and well-prepared warriors, but from that

---

[34] Psalm 91:1-2

moment on, they were uncovered and unprotected, as they would be fighting against the Lord.

Joshua and Caleb were not being simplistic and were most definitely not ignoring this crucial detail. But their words were emphasizing their confidence in God's promises and their certainty the He would guide them. By believing in God, both were sure that they would be fighting under His own *protection*.

These descendants of Anak could well have been a great and powerful people, but not more than the God of Caleb and Joshua. And while their cities might have been well-fortified, it would be the Israelites' own tents that would come to be established in that land. Maybe the giants indeed saw them as mere bugs, but without the Lord's *support*, they had become vulnerable, and it would be they who would be devoured like bread.

02 What You See is What You Believe

The rocket of our life is off the pad. Action is forever. We are becoming who we will be—forever.
Dallas Willard

Jesus was not a whisperer. No one ever saw Him close to His neighbor's ear, looking stealthily around lest some one should overhear what He was going to say. He stood upright, looked men squarely and kindly in the eye, and spoke what He had to say right out, boldly, frankly, that the whole world might hear; and when He did speak privately to His disciples, He told them to shout it from the housetops. 'Truth fears nothing but concealment,' said an old Church Father, and Jesus spoke only the truth.
Samuel Logan Brengle

The terrifying image of Canaan described by the ten spies had a devastating effect on the people's morale. With their powerful and persuasive words, these men had been sufficiently convincing as to change the course and destiny of many thousands of lives. It is truly impressive how the Israelites were led to believe the report given by those men rather than God's promises. They were like the *"sheeple"* of our times, those who are easily swayed by the current popular opinion and follow it without question.

I get the impression some people let themselves be convinced far more easily than others, possibly either due to mental apathy or weakness of character. Their minds lay bare, merely a blank canvas where anything may be projected, or like open soil ready to receive every kind of seed. Indeed, they have an obvious lack of conviction—a conviction which would serve as firm roots against the prevailing winds of uncertainty.

On the other hand, there are people who have the power of persuasion, easily convincing others to agree with their ideas and conclusions. They use people to give legitimacy to their beliefs and to justify their own actions, all with the goal of furthering their plans at the expense of others. These things require from us not only conviction but also discernment, so that we might not be as easily swayed by their schemes and led to sin against God.

With so much at stake, including the eternal destiny of our souls, the secret to combat these seductive plots is the assurance only a mature faith can provide. Though the

Devil and many others may want to take advantage of our minds, we find confidence in the constant renewal brought about by God's Word. Through it, we will come to know His perfect will, and we will be kept safe.[35]

Understanding God's will is a long but magnificent journey that, given enough time and discipline, slowly strengthens our relationship with Him. And just like in any other relationship, a friendship with the Lord also necessitates growth. Many times, a friendship may start out in tentative or timidly, with each person knowing little of the other. But given enough time and effort, a friendship becomes something to be enjoyed and savored, ultimately turning indispensable. This same Lord Jesus that invites us to come to know him is the one that called his disciples his friends and shared with them what he heard from the Father.[36]

God wishes for us to come to know and love Him, and the way He revealed Himself in Christ is the biggest proof of this. He goes on to say to the prophet Hosea He was not looking for sacrifices and burnt offerings, but rather for people who knew and loved Him.[37] The more we get to know Him, the more our eyes of faith will be uncovered. Only then can appreciate His beauty, and only

---

35 Romans 12:1-2
36 Hosea 6:6; John 15:15
37 Hosea 6:6

then—in an enrapturing and inevitable manner—can we surrender to Him.

Jesus is irresistible, but we first need to know Him to surrender to Him. Only then will see the obstacles of the soul disappear and be free to obey Him.

Knowing God should be the number one priority in our lives. A Christian firm in their faith won't be swept away by whoever speaks loudest, seems more intelligent or is most friendly. Scripture advises us to dedicate ourselves to knowing Christ until we can reach maturity of faith. The letter that the apostle Paul writes to the church in Ephesus relates very well to the story of how the Israelites were struck with fear:

> Until we all reach unity in the faith and in the knowledge of the Son of God and become mature, attaining to the whole measure of the fullness of Christ. Then we will no longer be infants, tossed back and forth by the waves, and blown here and there by every wind of teaching and by the cunning and craftiness of people in their deceitful scheming.[38]

---

[38] Ephesians 4:13-14

It is intriguing to see how the speech made by the spies seems to intensify in its description, almost to the point of absurdity, following Caleb's interference. They interrupt him with an immediate "But," and go on to emphasize the dangers and obstacles they would have to face, shifting their attention away from the rewards that this potential conquest would offer. They insisted on the difficulties they would need to overcome, should the leaders still decide to go on with the original plan (against their clear recommendation). The Hebrew word used here by the incredulous spies, דִּבָּה, dibo, means to defame, vilify, or slander against. In other words, they were giving this land an unreasonably harsh and malicious report.[39]

The assertion that the land's native inhabitants were powerful giants which would devour them whole was nothing more than ill-intentioned, fanciful exaggeration. Regardless, this lie quickly infected the Israelites with such fear that it completely paralyzed the whole camp. The people began to weep and cry loudly in a clear state of utter distress, rendering any possibility of rational or coherent thinking improbable at best.

The vivid details presented in the report not only gave the ten spies an aspect of authority, but also led the others to question the viability of their plans to conquer the Promised Land. Indeed, it is much easier to believe a lie when it is coated by a sprinkling of truth. Their report

---

[39] Numbers 13:32

wasn't a complete lie but a half-truth, which, at the end of the day, is still a lie. Every falsehood needs at least a little bit of truth mixed in at first to be believed until the end, and it was this strategy that the incredulous spies used. They began their report with true statements, then slowly began to add fabrications until, by the end of it, they had completely defamed the land.

> *"What is truth?" Pilate asked. Maybe he simply misheard, as Jesus had said shortly before, "I am the truth."*

Ironically, the fact that these spies had spread slander about the Promised Land and imbued fear in the heart of their own people, made them the true enemies of the Israelites – not these supposed giants. Their foes were not on the other side, across the border, but rather among them. It was the spies' devious words that prevented that generation from taking hold of the blessings the Lord had prepared for them. And now, with the people's minds worried about giants, the spies' deception was never found out.

We often blame external factors or find scapegoats for the difficulties we face, but the truth is that many times we ourselves are the source of these problems. However, to recognize this issue, we must make a concerted effort to humble ourselves and look inward, requiring great integrity and strength of character.

You are likely aware that the Bible states that Satan is our main enemy. It is written that he is the father of lies, and is an assassin and deceiver, among other titles.[40] The apostle Peter describes him as a "roaring lion", ready to seize and devour us at any opportunity.[41] Elsewhere, Paul writes that our battle is against "the rulers of darkness."[42] This is true, of course, and we most certainly have a powerful enemy entirely set on destroying us and driving us as far away from God as possible. We cannot ignore that, in many situations, we are responsible for our own destruction.

Consider the case of when Adam and Eve sinned and rebelled against God. When God came down and confronted them, they each blamed the other first until God pointed out who really was at fault. Adam spoke first and claimed that it was the fault of the woman that God had given him. In this statement, Adam was not only blaming the woman, but he was also blaming God for giving him the woman in the first place. Eve then protested and claimed that it was not her fault but the

---

[40] John 8:44
[41] 1 Peter 5:8
[42] Ephesians 6:12

serpent's. In the end, God passed judgment on all three of them, giving each of them a sentence.[43]

In this example, there really was an external enemy in the character of the serpent. However, the narrative places the emphasis on the offer given by the serpent, where the forbidden tree appeared to be "good for food, and that it was pleasant to the eyes, and a tree to be desired to make one wise".[44] Here we see that the Devil preyed upon the cravings of the man and the woman, a soil he found fertile to plant his destructive scheme. This is what James, the brother of Christ, describes as the common pattern of sin:

> But each person is tempted when they are dragged away by their own evil desire and enticed. Then, after desire has conceived, it gives birth to sin; and sin, when it is full-grown, gives birth to death.[45]

Ultimately, it was the Israelites' scarcity of faith that brought them to fall. Their hesitation—a sign of spiritual immaturity—was used against them at a moment where faith was most needed. Though they felt like mere bugs going up against the supposed giants across the border, the true giant they had to face was the fear inside themselves. This giant was far bigger and more powerful than any warrior they would face in Canaan. Likewise, though this giant may not make us physically weak, it

---

[43] Genesis 3:12-19
[44] Genesis 3:6
[45] James 1:14-15

strips us of the ability to act, suppressing our spirits, and by extension, our faith.

Israel had experienced the Lord's deliverance first-hand countless times and knew they could rely on Him. Yet, in their spiritual weakness, they created a competition between God and the Canaanites. Certainly, God was far more powerful than all their warriors and chariots combined, but in their indecisiveness, blinded by fear, Israel chose neither God nor the giants. Instead, they chose themselves, or rather, the fear that weighed them down. Their fear acted like an anchor, preventing them from freely sailing on the river of life God offered them. The giants, however, were presented as the winners for Israel to have someone to blame.

It is common knowledge that, whenever we need to make a weighty decision, we should analyse all the relevant information beforehand to aim for the best possible outcome. Equally as important is to ensure that this information is dependable and trustworthy. No one in their right mind would deliberately sabotage themselves by making decisions based on inaccurate information. However, a factor we may overlook in our decision-making is the factor of God. Not only do we need to verify the credibility of the available information, but also to consider Him in all our decisions. The Israelites did neither: they neither had credible information nor considered God in their operation.

In the hour of decision, lay all the factors on the table, and naturally, do not leave out the "God factor". The difference is eternal!

For years, the Lord had been repeating his promise He would one day free Israel from their bonds and lead them to a place of abundance and riches. Not only had God promised this to their patriarch Abraham many years before, but also many times to this very group of people since their deliverance from Egypt until their arrival at Kadesh:

> I have indeed seen the misery of my people in Egypt. I have heard them crying out because of their slave drivers, and I am concerned about their suffering. So, I have come down to rescue them from the hand of the Egyptians and to bring them up out of that land into a good and spacious land, a land flowing with milk and honey—the home of the Canaanites, Hittites, Amorites, Perizzites, Hivites and Jebusites. (Exodus 3:7-8)

> I have seen what has been done to you in Egypt. And I have promised to bring you up out of your misery in Egypt into the land of the Canaanites, Hittites, Amorites, Perizzites, Hivites and Jebusites—a land flowing with milk and honey.' (Exodus 3:16-17)

> When the Lord brings you into the land of the Canaanites, Hittites, Amorites, Hivites and Jebusites—the land he swore to your ancestors to give you, a land flowing with milk and honey. (Exodus 13:5)

> Leave this place, you and the people you brought up out of Egypt and go up to the land I promised on oath to Abraham, Isaac and Jacob, saying, 'I will give it to your descendants.' I will send an angel before you and drive out the Canaanites, Amorites, Hittites, Perizzites, Hivites and Jebusites. Go up to the land flowing with milk and honey. (Exodus 33.1-3)

> You will possess their land; I will give it to you as an inheritance, a land flowing with milk and honey." I am the Lord your God, who has set you apart from the nations. (Leviticus 20:24)

God had taken constant care to remind them of the original covenant He had made with Abraham. The events described here in Numbers chapters 13 and 14, and Deuteronomy chapter 1, all take place only a few miles from Hebron, the exact location where the Lord had made the original promise to Abraham.[46] In fact, the spies had passed through that very same area as part of their incursion into the Promised Land. Those twelve men had walked exactly where Abraham had stood many centuries before.

---

46 Genesis 13:14-18

It is not mere coincidence that this rebellion unfolded right at the gates of where Abraham and his son Isaac had lived. It was from here that Abraham had come out in defense of his nephew Lot against the kings who had kidnapped him.[47] The Bible mentions the burial of Sarah, Abraham's wife, at a place called Kiriath-Arba, which is in Hebron of Canaan, in the cave of Machpelah. Years later, Abraham, and subsequently, his son Isaac and grandson Jacob, were buried there.[48]

Despite knowing this, Israel preferred to doubt God's ability to securely give them that land. Certainly, many intimidating obstacles would come up along the way, but God's faithfulness was not lacking evidence.

I believe there was a certain tone of irony in God's voice as He spoke to Moses authorizing the dispatch of the twelve spies. Years later, we see Moses again, this time speaking in his final words, admitting he had been convinced by the other leaders on the importance of sending out that expedition beforehand. God's original plan did not involve this step at all, and He had already declared He would give them that land. In authorizing the use of the spies, God said He would send them to the land *"which I am giving to the Israelites"*.[49]

---

47 Genesis 14:12-17
48 Genesis 23:2, 19; 29.9; 35.29; 50.13
49 Numbers 13:2

> *Without God, all plans are in vain, fleeting like vapor in the wind. The best plan is to follow God's plan.*

In an interview with a popular radio station in the US, pastor and author Max Lucado, comments on one of his books by arguing that when we nourish our faith, our fears all die of hunger. He continues by saying that the reverse is also true: if we feed our fears, then our faith will starve. Finally, he concludes by stating that the problem is in "our tendency to feed our fears. We need to be intentional in nourishing our faith."[50] Our lives will mirror whatever we allow into our minds. As the Roman emperor and philosopher Marcus Aurelius writes in his book *Meditations*, "your soul takes on the color of your thoughts".[51]

Unfortunately, the people of Israel chose to feed their fears and believe the words of men rather than God's. "The people are stronger and taller than we are; the cities are large, with walls up to the sky," they said to themselves.[52] To them, the giants seemed far more powerful than God, and there was nothing He could do

---

[50] Max Lucado, "Fearless", 2009, Thomas Nelson Publishing

[51] Marcus Aurelius, Meditations, Book V, verse 16. Translation by Gregory Hays, 2003

[52] Deuteronomy 1:26-28

to help them. Fear in their hearts caused their perception of God to greatly diminish. God's true character and His plans for them were twisted and confused in such a way that they, again, preferred to suppress the truth and believe in injustice, fear, and lies. That which had been made abundantly clear by God was questioned, negated, tainted, and finally rejected.[53]

Perhaps, in their minds, the unthinkable had happened: God had stale and outdated information about the land, while the spies, having visited it recently, knew more about its current state of affairs than He did. Maybe the giants had been a surprise to God: a hitherto unknown fact to Him. Or perhaps God had simply forgotten about them or did not notice them when He first made the promise to Abraham all those years ago. Maybe the giants arrived only recently, throwing a wrench into an old and outdated plan. Whatever the case, the giants were now there, and they had grown to be a mighty and invincible army. Surely, this would force God to change His plans, as times have changed and God should have known better.

Leo Tolstoy, the great 19th century Russian author, writes how a wrong never ceases to be wrong simply because a majority share in it. Indeed, how many people's opinions would it take to supersede God's truth? Would a petition containing one million signatures be sufficient

---

[53] Romans 1.8

to overthrow His divine decrees? What if we included the support of mainstream media, governments, and social media influencers? Would we then become confident enough to not only install a new moral standard in our society but to also "update" the Bible itself?

This is exactly what the Israelites were doing when they tried to stone Moses, Caleb, and Joshua. It was a way of silencing them—of silencing God Himself and putting their own words—our own words—in the pages of His unchanging Scripture. And the fact of the matter was that the new "truth" brought about by the ten spies was enough to both simultaneously erase God's word from the people's minds and to inflict fear in their hearts. This misplaced fear of the giants then made them lose the correct and righteous fear: the fear of the Lord. What a contradiction! And, sadly, more common than what we might think. How many times do we face an apparent giant only for it to be revealed as a mere dwarf behind smoke and mirrors later on? Thus, instead of fearing the real Giant, the Lord who loves us, we fear the oppressor.

So, since the people were so sure that the spies knew more than God did, He conceded to their request. It did not matter that the Lord had already given them the orders He would "give the land to [them]", as in their minds, the spies' report had clearly debunked God's authority. Their depraved desires had their way, and this report had given them the perfect excuse to dishonor the Lord. They now decided what was right and what was wrong. It all was an expected twist that led them to a big inversion of values, where allegiance existed only to the self and wrong became right—it became the norm.

When fear takes hold of our minds, we must be ready to fight it. The best weapon we can use against it is the Word of God, which constantly reminds us of His love. In psalm 119, the poet recognizes the importance of knowing God's Word by saying, "I seek you with all my heart; do not let me stray from your commands. I have hidden your word in my heart that I might not sin against you".[54] Martin Luther, the Protestant reformer, said that while we cannot prevent the birds flying over our heads, we can certainly prevent them from making nests there. While we are all subject to the advances of fear, the great question is whether we will allow it to overcome us.

Indeed, fear can increase the apparent size of any obstacle, turning it into an impenetrable barrier. Just as the spies embellished their report, going as far as including false information, so too can we run the risk of believing in things that may or may not be real, or seeing problems much bigger and tougher than they actually are.

The Roman philosopher, Seneca, argued that we have a much greater tendency to suffer with things that are merely in our imagination, rather than on things based in reality; while Paul reminds us that we need to focus our attention on things that are true, noble, correct, pure,

---

54 Psalm 119:10-11

lovely, and admirable. These are the things that should always occupy our minds, things that are excellent and praiseworthy, he continues.[55] Paul himself said to the church in Corinth that his main concern was to capture the minds of his readers, and desired to "take captive every thought to make it obedient to Christ."[56]

Faith is always present, but the question is what we base our faith on. To make their decision, the Israelites had to believe, either in the spies' report, that the so-called giants of Canaan were unbeatable - despite never having seen them, or in the words of Joshua and Caleb about the promises of God.

Such disposition, one of a mind filled by the Holy Spirit, would have certainly made all the difference in the Israelites' history. They would have trusted God's promises and would not have seen the inhabitants of Canaan as an impossible enemy. Those men and women would have known that the Lord had given them that land

---

[55] Philippians 4:8
[56] 2 Corinthians 10:5

and blessed them with the privilege of being the generation to finally fulfill the promise made to Abraham so many years earlier.

An effective way of visualizing the process of nourishing our faith is to imagine an armory, the space where an army's weapons and munitions are stored. In those most critical moments of life, the arsenal at our disposal is stocked entirely by whatever we have stored up in our hearts and minds. We can only use the things we have at our disposal, whether they be good or bad, powerful, or not. Regardless of our beliefs, values, or convictions, these are the things that will be manifest in our times of need. They will surface and become visible to others in the form of our reactions to times of trouble. All we have put into our minds will be there, stocked, and ready to be used at the opportune moment. As such, our ability to respond will always be in accordance with our spiritual arsenal, whether it be faith in God or faith in fear.

Just like our bodies, our souls also require daily nourishment. We need to constantly remind it on the reasons for our faith, lest the Devil succeed in making us forget them.

To put it simply, the way we react is based upon what we have made abundant in our hearts. This all depends on whether we have built our lives trusting human fallacies or the voice of God. Jesus, in fact, reminds us that His sheep know His voice,[57] and that this intimacy with the Lord and His Word should be the goal for our souls.

There is an excerpt in the book, The Chronicles of Narnia, which gives us an example on recognizing the voice of God. Lucy, Edmund, Eustace, and Caspian sailed towards what they believed to be an island. As they approached, however, they discovered that it was a great darkness. The bow of the ship was dark and everyone on board was terrified and desperate. Until something flew over the ship's mast and a noise was heard. No one understood what was going on except Lucy. As it circled the mast, a voice whispered to her: "Courage, dear heart!", and the voice, she felt sure, was Aslan's, and "with the voice a delicious smell breathed in her face."[58] Over time, that voice became familiar to Lucy's ears, who could pick it out in any situation.

We need to surrender to what God says. Through His Word, we too can experience the same power that has created, sustained, and transformed lives throughout history. It was like that with Joshua. When he was given the enormous challenge of replacing Moses at the head of the people of Israel, he was instructed to hold fast to the

---

[57] John 10:27-29
[58] CS. Lewis. The Voyage of the Dawn Treader. H. Collins, 1994, p. 187

Law of God; not to depart from it; not stop talking about it and meditating on it day and night.[59] In the face of that extraordinary mission, God's strategic plan for the new leader was very clear: Hold fast to my Word. That still holds true for us today.

Whenever faced with a serious or uncertain situation, we have the incredible opportunity to enjoy an unmistakable peace only Christ can offer. Whenever fear enters a heart filled with faith in God, it is quickly brought before Christ, who, instead, fills it with peace. Someone who has, along the years, dedicated themselves to knowing the Lord, will have learned perseverance and good spirits, always being able to maintain hope.[60]

Despite the words *fear* and *faith* regularly showing up together in the same sentence, Jesus' reprimand to His cowardly disciples on the boat during a storm is, at least to me, a most intimidating example. The Gospels tell us that as Jesus slept on the boat, the waves began to crash against it, threatening to sink it. The expert fishermen then began to cry out in fear, "Lord, save us! We are going to drown!" Jesus' reply to them is not easily digestible, "You of little faith, why are you so afraid?"[61] Notice how chillingly close the words *fear* and *faith* are to each other,

---

[59] Joshua 1:7-9
[60] Romans 15:4
[61] Matthew 8:26

in the very same sentence. It demonstrates just how little His disciples trusted their Master's care.

This event on that boat with Jesus and His disciples clearly demonstrates the correlation between fear and faith, with one having influence over the other. In a later episode, for example, Jesus praises a Canaanite woman for her faith in believing His power to heal her suffering daughter.[62] Similarly, the apostle Paul rejoiced in hearing that the church in Thessalonica in Greece had a faith continuously "growing more and more."[63] Indeed, the rate at which our faith grows is directly proportional to the rate in which we nourish our relationship with Christ.

When Jesus tells us not to fear, He is inviting us to trust Him. If He is on your boat, even the seas will obey.

It is this same Lord that calmed the sea who wishes to calm the greatest storm of our lives. Our perturbed soul is unable to find rest despite its unending and intermittent search. Its existential uncertainties and restlessness that assault it reveal its true state of frailty. Despite its courageous search, it knows deep down that it is

---

[62] Matthew 15:28
[63] 2 Thessalonians 1:3

precarious and cannot find meaning for life or death on its own. If tis state of restlessness is disheartening, Jesus' invitation is a breath of fresh air, bringing relief to a weary soul. The soul needs not fight alone.

True rest will only come when we anchor our hearts in the safe harbor that is Christ. "God is light; in Him there is no darkness at all,"[64] is a message that should spark in the believer a revolution of peace. By having all darkness vanish before His marvelous light, we can have the "assurance that His universe is a perfectly safe place for us to be,"[65] as Dallas Willard once said.

In the end, faith is the ultimate factor for us being able to enjoy this level of confidence. Having faith is required. Period. And I am not saying merely believing that Jesus was just a historical person, or a role model—a great master of morality, as a colleague of mine once put it. What I mean is believing He was indeed God, and that only He can bring life to our dead hearts. "You must make your choice," challenges C.S. Lewis, "Either this man was, and is, the Son of God: or else a madman or something worse. You can shut Him up for a fool, you can spit at Him and kill Him as a demon; or you can fall at His feet and call Him Lord and God."[66]

---

[64] 1 John 1:5
[65] Dallas Willard, The Divine Conspiracy, HarperCollins, 1998, p. 321
[66] C.S. Lewis, Selected Books, HarperCollins, 1999, p. 353.

Only faith in the Son of God will bring peace to our hearts. Every corner of our minds should be filled with Christ, completely engulfed by our glorious God. The more we allow His Words to enter our hearts, the more we will experience spiritual stability and courage, as He himself promises: "Peace I leave with you; my peace I give you. I do not give to you as the world gives. Do not let your hearts be troubled and do not be afraid."[67] If we know the Word of God and place our faith in it, then we can repeat King David's own words: The Lord is my light and my salvation; whom shall I fear? The Lord is the stronghold of my life; of whom shall I be afraid?[68]

We likely won't know all the details of God's promises for us, but we need to be ready to surrender our faith to His love. Even if we are going through terrible battles and seemingly never-ending trials, God promises us to use them for our ultimate good.

When we come to understand His ultimate objective is to mold us in the image of His Son Jesus,[69] it gives us peace to confront any tribulation. He is the God who turns evil into good.[70] It is possible that we may not see good happening in our lives at that very moment, but we can be certain that God knows the outcome and rejoices in it.

---

[67] John 14:27
[68] Psalm 27:1
[69] Romans 8.28
[70] Genesis 50:20

03 High-Impact Connections

Brave men are vertebrates; they have their softness on the surface and their toughness in the middle. But these modern cowards are all crustaceans; their hardness is all on the cover and their softness is inside.
G. K. Chesterton

Who knows not Love, let him assay
And taste that juice which, on the cross, a pike
Did set again abroach; then let him say
If ever he did taste the like,
Love is that liquor sweet and most divine,
Which my God feels as blood, but I as wine.
George Herbert

Now faced with a popular revolt, God raises a question to Moses: "How long will these people treat me with contempt? How long will they refuse to believe in me, despite all the signs I have performed among them?"[71] As Moses later writes, God had walked alongside the Israelites faithfully since the very beginning, being their Provider in every circumstance:

> After leaving Sukkoth they camped at Etham on the edge of the desert. By day the Lord went ahead of them in a pillar of cloud to guide them on their way and by night in a pillar of fire to give them light, so that they could travel by day or night. Neither the pillar of cloud by day nor the pillar of fire by night left its place in front of the people.[72]

God had powerfully delivered them from the hand of Pharaoh in Egypt, led them in the crossing of the Red Sea in a manner thought impossible, nourished them in the desert with bread (manna) and quail, and spouted for them water out of bare rock. All this was done in addition to directly revealing His will in the form of the Ten Commandments atop Mount Sinai. Considering all these acts of providence, it is hard to imagine a single other group in history that had experienced God's presence in such a powerful and personal manner. God also had personally guaranteed Moses He would guide them until

---

[71] Numbers 14:11
[72] Exodus 13:20-22

the very end of the journey: "My Presence will go with you, and I will give you rest."[73]

Even after experiencing so many miracles, perhaps to the point of becoming *accustomed* to them, Israel had disregarded the God of those miracles, preferring to put their faith in fear and trusting in its voice instead. Former US president Franklin Roosevelt once said that the only thing we should fear is fear itself, in the sense that being afraid of fear is a necessity. When we are afraid, fear attempts to overcome us; our senses are distorted, and our reasoning is compromised. As a consequence, any action that could change the course of a story remains paralyzed.

We all fear. After all, fear is a sign of our own humanity; that we are not made of iron, and much less gods.

Fear can be extremely effective. Acting in an instinct of self-preservation serves as a catalyst for much of the comfort, well-being, and safety humanity enjoys today. This instinct cannot be allowed to grow beyond a mere

---

[73] Exodus 33:14

natural reaction, as it would become an obstacle to our personal adventures and conquests.

Consider, for example, one of the most energetic warriors in the biblical narrative, David. There came a time in the life of the future king of Israel where he had been captured by the Philistines while escaping the armies of the current king of Israel, Saul.[74] This was a moment in which David came to experience true fear, as the situation was extremely difficult and precarious. It was then that he wrote Psalm 56, a sincere prayer that outlines his fears and his decision to trust in God. Notice how his words are filled with fear:

> Be merciful to me, my God, for my enemies are in hot pursuit; all day long they press their attack. My adversaries pursue me all day long; in their pride many are attacking me. All day long they twist my words; all their schemes are for my ruin. They conspire, they lurk, they watch my steps, hoping to take my life.[75]

Those were certainly terrifying days for David, where any moment, he thought, could well be his last. Despite this exceedingly dangerous situation, filled with excessive adrenaline, more than once in this psalm he says, "I am not afraid."[76] I believe it was through his faith in God that David confronted these challenges.

---

74 1 Samuel 21
75 Psalm 56:1-2, 5-6
76 Psalm 56:4, 11

> When I am afraid, I put my trust in you. In God, whose word I praise—in God I trust and am not afraid. What can mere mortals do to me?[77]

David was sincere in recognizing the reality of the danger and fear around him; he did not ignore them. On the contrary, he began his prayer by saying, "When I am afraid". This was simply a poetic way of confessing, "I *am* afraid." We should not be surprised when fear knocks at the doors of our hearts, as that is inevitable. The real question is what we do with it once it is here. David does not remain afraid for long, stating, "When I am afraid, I put my trust in you."

We are weak and vulnerable, even in times of peace, when the difficulties of life seem far away and distant. The Bible never refers to us as men of steel, but as dust, or as fog and dew that covers the hillside.[78] We should be relieved to hear even a warrior as powerful and strong as David also became afraid. It is perfectly normal to be afraid, but the difference lies in where we turn to in those moments. The apostle Peter gives us clear direction: "Cast all your anxiety on him because he cares for you."[79]

---

[77] Psalm 56:3-4
[78] Psalm 103:13-14
[79] 1 Peter 5:7

In contrast to fear, it is faith in God that leads us to the important conquests of life, with the most crucial of these being life itself.

David *had* such a confidence, throwing himself upon the arms of the Lord to find rest from his fears. We must remember that David could only do this because he knew the Lord. His relationship with God and His Word were the basis for such a conviction: "In God, whose word I praise, in the Lord, whose word I praise—in God I trust and am not afraid. What can man do to me?"[80] And fortunately for us, such a relationship is within our reach.

The countless adventures David experienced almost always tested his courage. Despite frequent trials, he never permitted fear to overcome him. An indicator to measure the how much fear has taken control of our hearts is to check how much it undermines our ability to face it or ignore it. Putting our faith in fear lets it guide our decisions and emotions.

Fear takes us to a realm of unknowns, filled with the non-existent and unexpected, "reaching its maximum

---

[80] Psalm 56:10-11

suffering in the face of nothingness"[81] and impossibility. Despite David's agonies and afflictions being real, he didn't find himself in a void, insecure and incapable. His faith allowed him to "walk before God in the light of life."[82]

Excessive worries not only imprison us, but also become a distraction and obstacle that rob us from the pleasure of enjoying life. It is inconsistent to live imprisoned by fear when we know that Christ has already set us free.[83] As such, instead of putting our faith in fear (i.e., driven by fear), we should reject it, not allowing it to grow and overcome us. Faith is meant to be in God alone.

Considering the Israelites' situation, their attitude was simply unjustifiable. The many signs they had experienced were physical proofs of God's power and presence. Another example was the fact that at that time, Israel had roughly 600,000 men ready for war, making them not quite as vulnerable as one might have thought. They could have been just as strong or even stronger than the Canaanites in sheer number alone. While we do not have an answer to that for sure, I cannot help but think what 600,000 men could do in a war with the God of Armies as their general. Is that not what Scripture

---

[81] Free translation of Emilio Mira y López. Cuatro Gigantes del Alma. Ediciones Lidiun, 1993, p. 123.

[82] Psalm 56:13

[83] Galatians 5:1

itself states, that nothing is too difficult for the Lord?[84] Regardless, Israel was simply not convinced they could win a battle against Canaan. So many miracles, yet they were not able to hold on to their faith, or at least not to the point of making it endure. One might argue that they had only a superficial faith in God, or that their understanding of God, notwithstanding His miracles in Egypt and in the desert, was utterly shallow.

Some relationships are toxic and harmful. They try to control us with blackmail and deception contrary to truth and common sense. If our friends cannot make us better people, then we must not allow them to make us worse.

The factor that most impacted Israel's decision was not the situation itself nor the miracles witnessed, but the influence of the ten unbelieving spies. Their fears and lies permeated the people to the point where they truly came to believe the Canaanite cities were too well fortified, too strongly built; with walls so tall not even God could breach them.

---

[84] Jeremiah 32:27

As it typically happens in such situations, their unbelief and distrust distorted their perception of God, leading them astray from reality. The spies achieved this by telling a story with *aspects* of truth, one of the most subtle tricks known. A half-truth is much easier to accept than a blatant lie. Christian author Os Guinness vividly and dramatically describes the hijacking of truth by lies:

> Sin and disobedience lay hold of truth, grasp it roughly, and will not let it be what it naturally is or say what it naturally says. In this way, the deliberate dynamic of unbelief is to suppress truth, stifle truth and hold truth hostage.[85]

Years later, Moses reminisces on how he tried to motivate his brothers, urging them not to give up:

> Do not be terrified; do not be afraid of them. The Lord your God, who is going before you, will fight for you, as he did for you in Egypt, before your very eyes, and in the wilderness. There you saw how the Lord your God carried you, as a father carries his son, all the way you went until you reached this place.[86]

Moses' words had little to no effect on them, just as the abundance of miraculous signs did not produce faith in the people. Israel also would not allow Moses' words of encouragement to move their hearts. Heaven observed this indifference with great indignation:

---

[85]Os Guinness, Fool's talk, IVP Books, 2015, p. 85.
[86] Deuteronomy 1.29-31

How long will these people treat me with contempt? How long will they refuse to believe in me, in spite of all the signs I have performed among them?[87]

The spies, on the other hand, had a devastating impact on the people. The hysteria was so great, they spent the night weeping and wailing loudly, crying out against Moses' and Aaron's leadership. It got to such a state the people declared they would have rather died in Egypt or the desert than be here only to be served as lunch to the giants. They even went as far as using their women and children as perfect excuses to derail the invasion of the Promised Land.

We can empathise with the sentiment of men who wanted to protect their families. Indeed, the instinct to protect our families is, for so many believers, understandably a step beyond the tolerable limit of a test of faith. It is not difficult to find those willing to support us when we put our faith aside to prioritize our children.

Many would agree that faith is only valid *so long as* it does not require of us those who we hold most dear. Even so, the Lord requires of us the utmost loyalty. Indeed, that is often the most significant test of our loyalty – especially when He wants to use those closest to us for His purposes.[88]

---

[87] Numbers 14.11
[88] Matthew 10.37; Luke 14.26

*Only when we love God above all things
will we be able to truly love all things.*

We all complain, and complaining can be very contagious. Whether it be in wisdom or in madness, when the whirlwind of the moment passes, it drags the crowd along with it. Thankfully, Caleb's household was not infected by this hysteria. Though he also had his own family, wife, and children to think about, he maintained the willingness to fight the battle: "We should go up and take possession of the land, for we can certainly do it!", was his challenge to the people.

As I compare Caleb's words with Moses', I realize how similar they really are. I can't help but notice the impact Moses had on Caleb, as Caleb's closeness to his leader led him to trust his words, character, and intentions. Caleb knew that the promises transmitted by Moses came directly from God: "Go up and take possession of it as the Lord, the God of your ancestors, told you. Do not be afraid; do not be discouraged."[89]

Caleb did not waste the opportunity given him. He allowed himself to be molded by his relationship with God and Moses. As God had personally guided His people through the desert, Caleb used every available

---

[89] Numbers 13.30; Deuteronomy 1.21

moment to come closer to the Lord; so much so that even God Himself declared that Caleb had a "different spirit" that followed Him "wholeheartedly".[90] In fact, this expression of "following God wholeheartedly", appears in the Bible no less than six times referring to Caleb's relationship with the Lord.[91]

The cultivation of faith requires habit, which in turn requires discipline. And the best way to exercise discipline is to share it in the company of those who want to cultivate the same faith.

The Bible speaks clearly about the importance of our personal relationships, and we know how great an impact they have in our development, including the friendships we cultivate. We are malleable beings with a capacity to be molded and shaped by those around us, just as we are capable of molding and impacting others.

The book of Proverbs uses the analogy of iron sharpening iron, as one sharpens a knife, to remind us of how we can shape the lives of others. That same book of biblical wisdom states that those who "walk with the wise

---

[90] Numbers 14:24
[91] Numbers 14:24, 32:12; Deuteronomy 1:36; Joshua 14:8-9, 14

[…] become wise, for a companion of fools suffers harm." Jesus identifies us as salt of the earth and light to the world, giving us a responsibility of utilizing our lives in the service of others. Paul, on the other hand, warns us that bad company can also corrupt us thoroughly.[92]

We always risk resembling those with whom we walk or that which we love. Our relationships influence our behavior, habits, thoughts, speech, and so on. This is why the psalmist says, "blessed is the one who does not walk in step with the wicked or stand in the way that sinners take or sit in the company of mockers."[93] For good company can bring out the best in us, maybe even things we did not know we had. The opposite is also true:

> A good man brings good things out of the good stored up in his heart, and an evil man brings evil things out of the evil stored up in his heart. For the mouth speaks what the heart is full of.[94]

How wonderful is it, then, to have good friends! Better still if they point us to God, encouraging us towards love and good works.[95] The Israelites had many friends, but they tragically allowed themselves to be infected by fear an unbelief. Moses clearly calls out the unbelieving spies for robbing the people's hearts from

---

[92] Prov. 27.17; Matth. 5.13-16, 1 Cor. 15.33, Prov. 13.20
[93] Psalm 1.1
[94] Luke 6.45
[95] Hebrews 10.24

faith and discouraging them from battle.[96] The verb "discouraged" used here in the original Hebrew is מָסַס, *masas*, and is sometimes translated as to "dissolve" or "melt"; which is exactly what happened to their hearts.

The fear present in the spies jumped from their hearts to those of the people, merging and coalescing, joining together as one big and fearful heart. Curiously, only two years before, shortly after their crossing of the Red Sea, they used another similar word, that being מוג, mug, when they sang out in praise to the Lord, saying that the "people of Canaan will *melt away*; terror and dread will fall on them."[97] Unfortunately, it was the Israelites themselves that ended up *melting away*. They stopped trusting in God and His Promises, destined now to be remembered only as those who faltered in the desert, at the gates of the Promised Land:

> Who were they who heard and rebelled? Were they not all those Moses led out of Egypt?... those who sinned, whose bodies perished in the wilderness? And to whom did God swear that they would never enter his rest if not to those who disobeyed? So, we see that they were not able to enter, because of their unbelief.[98]

---

[96] Deuteronomy 1.28
[97] Exodus 15.14-18
[98] Hebrews 3.16-18

04 Consequences of Fear and Faith

I own myself wretched–aye thrice wretched. I am guilty of many errors. Through faith alone I look for finding some mercy in the day of the Lord's appearing.
Chrysostom

To dare is to lose one's footing momentarily.
Not to dare is to lose oneself.
Soren Kierkegaard

The walk of faith is like going up an invisible staircase. When you have climbed and climbed, you sometimes cannot see one single step before you. Each step seems to be upon the air, and yet when you put your foot down it is solid granite firmer than the earth itself.
Charles Spurgeon

It is well known that actions we take carry with them consequences, be they good or bad. So, it does not take much to reason that Israel's stubborn refusal to trust in the Lord would surely cost them dearly: "How long will these people treat me with contempt?", asked the Lord unto Moses. Their lack of faith had wedged itself between God and His eternal plans for them, and, as sin always does, eventually lead them to death. But despite this apparent setback, God would continue with His plans to turn Israel into a powerful nation, far beyond that of this unfaithful generation.[99]

Faith is fundamental to a strong relationship with the Lord, and, by extension, serves as the basis on which we may build a life ultimately worth living. To have faith is to enable ourselves to see life through a new lens, one especially adjusted by our trust in Him, making it possible for us to see things we would otherwise miss. And it is only by faith we can truly understand that everything, as the Bible says, solely exists by God's command. Therefore, it is the basis for a relationship with Him. If we do not believe He exists and has left His will recorded in the Scriptures, then nothing else about Him makes sense.

To believe in God is not simply to believe in His existence, but it is also to recognize His divinity and sovereignty. Further still, to believe in such a supreme

---

God also implies we accept His commands and act according to His word. To believe is to trust in what He has promised, submitting to His will, and obeying His orders. This profound conviction is then rewarded by access to Him. The free offer of salvation God offers can only be received by faith when we accept His promises. It is through faith we are accounted righteous, and by faith alone we can live eternally.[100]

Our choices should not reflect our fears, but our trust in the Lord. Confidence breeds courage and boldness.

The author of the book of Hebrews clearly says it was because of unbelief that the Israelites could not enter the Promised Land.[101] The question was not who was stronger, had a more powerful army, or was better prepared for war; nor was it whether they could defeat the enemy at all. The only requirement expected of them was to trust that God would keep His promises and to give them the land—and in this they failed.

When God said He would destroy the people with a plague and disinherit them from Abraham's inheritance,

[100] Genesis 15:6; Romans 1:16-17; Hebrews 11:1-6
[101] Hebrews 3:19

it was not an irrational or unreasonable reaction on His part. God is just; therefore, His verdicts are always just.[102] So, the Lord established judgement on that unfaithful generation for their sin of not trusting in the assurance He would lead them to that rich and abundant land. The Israelites had stopped trusting in what He had said, exchanging His truth for the lies and false accusations brought by those ten spies.

Their trail of sin did not stop there. The people sinned by attempting to kill Caleb and Joshua—indeed, *attempted*, as they would have definitely done so without divine intervention. They sinned by wanting to pick a new leader—one to bring them back to Egypt—and by doing so, rejected the leadership chosen by God in Moses. They sinned by choosing Egypt instead of Canaan. They sinned by going as far as preferring to die in the desert than to live in that land.

After so much sin and countless opportunities for repentance, God decided that those people should die. No one would inherit the land until a new generation arose to take it in their place. But had it not been for Moses' intervention, their destruction would have been imminent. Despite being rejected by Israel as their leader, Moses was still able to intercede for them humbly and courageously. He argued with the Lord by asking what other nations might think about the God who destroyed

---

102 Psalm 145:17

His own people. Moses even appealed to His character: patient and faithful, always ready to forgive. He knew intimately well the God to whom he prayed:

> In accordance with your great love, forgive the sin of these people, just as you have pardoned them from the time they left Egypt until now.[103]

As leader of the Hebrews, Moses had built such an intimate relationship with the Lord that he was fully able to trust in all His mercies. He knew God could forgive them, and thus pleaded in their place. By analogy, Moses is analogous to Christ, who, although rejected and nailed to a cross, prayed for those who had put him there.[104] Moses then prayed to God, "in such anguish, [that] there was nothing left but to pour out his desires before God."[105]

James tells us the prayer of the righteous has great power,[106] and, sure enough, the Lord listened to Moses' pleas. "I have forgiven them, as you asked,"[107] was the Lord's reply. God then presented His new plan to Moses, saying that although they were forgiven and He would not exterminate the Israelites at once, they would still suffer the consequences for their sins. As such, that

---

[103] Numbers 14:19
[104] Luke 23:34
[105] John Calvin
[106] James 5:16
[107] Numbers 14:20

generation would no longer be allowed to enter the Promised Land.

In the days following their rebellion, the people were instructed to leave their encampment near Canaan and to resume their pilgrimage in the desert. This time, however, their goal was not to reach a specific place, but instead, a specific state of being: death. They were to wander the desert until that entire generation had died out. Only then would the next generation, that of their children, receive the inheritance. Hence, we see God handing out His judgement accordingly, fit for the deeds of each individual, be they guilty or innocent, righteous, or unrighteous.

With every decision we make, we come ever closer to a final state of being, all in pursuit of a desired ideal or goal. Like bricks placed on top of each other, every decision builds up the whole a little more. Are we, then, building bridges or walls in our relationship with God?

God had heard the murmuring of the Israelites even when they whispered within the confines of their tents.

The words they spoke against Moses and the Lord Himself were not hidden from His ears. And though the Israelites had been deaf to the voice of God, God had certainly not been deaf to theirs: "I have heard the complaints of these grumbling Israelites", and, "As surely as I live, declares the Lord, I will do to you the very thing I heard you say."[108]

In their rebellion against the Lord, the Hebrews complained that it would have been better if they had simply died in the desert[109], so God granted them their wish.[110] Their will would be done starting from the next morning, where they would walk the desert until they all perished. These rebels would then die exactly how and where they wanted. Further adding to the irony, they would die right next to the land of freedom they could most certainly have enjoyed.

God's will truly is amazing, but many times, we unfortunately insist on doing things according to our own will instead of His. What a tragic moment it is then, when God gives us up to our own will[111]. C.S. Lewis ably noted how men are separated into two groups: "There are only two kinds of people in the end: those who say

---

108 Numbers 14:27-29
109 Numbers 14:2
110 Numbers 14:32-35
111 Romans 1:28-32

to God, 'Thy will be done,' and those to whom God says, in the end, 'Thy will be done.'"

So, God ruled that the punishment for the Israelites would be 40 years in the desert, until that whole generation had died out: one year for each of the 40 days that the spies had spent exploring the land. This sentence would serve as a process of education, teaching them about the consequences of their choices. "Simply don't rebel against the Lord," Caleb advised the people. Nowhere in this entire episode do we see a suggestion of anything or anyone that could have prevented the Israelites from owning that land, other than their rebellion against the Lord. Thus, rebellion truly was and still is a terrible and highly provocative sin.[112]

In addition to the sentence given to the guilty in the rebellion, God treated the ten unfaithful spies even more harshly. Because they had slandered the land God had chosen and then proceeded to provoke the people to rebel against the Lord, these spies were immediately put to death. While the remainder of the people were to wait for their ultimate end in the desert naturally, these spies were punished as an example before all:

> So, the men Moses had sent to explore the land, who returned and made the whole community grumble against him by spreading a bad report about it— these men who were responsible for spreading the bad

---

112 1 Samuel 15:23

> report about the land were struck down and died of a plague before the LORD. Of the men who went to explore the land, only Joshua son of Nun and Caleb son of Jephunneh survived.[113]

After dealing with those responsible in leading the rebellion, we can then see the care God had for the innocent. At the height of their revolt, the people had claimed they could not fight the giants for the sake of their children. Their excuse for not carrying out God's command seemed sensible in their eyes; after all, these giants were sure to capture them and make them and their children their slaves:

> As for your children that you said would be taken as plunder, I will bring them in to enjoy the land you have rejected. But as for you, your bodies will fall in this wilderness. Your children will be shepherds here for forty years, suffering for your unfaithfulness, until the last of your bodies lies in the wilderness. For forty years—one year for each of the forty days you explored the land—you will suffer for your sins and know what it is like to have me against you."[114]

God was stating that their excuse was an affront to His ability to protect His people and to keep His promises. God makes a point of clearly telling them that, in His sovereignty, He, and He alone, is the final upholder of our lives. And, unfortunately, many times,

---

[113] Numbers 14:36-38
[114] Numbers 14:3, 29, 31, 33

we tend to forget this. We take control of our children's lives while ignoring the fact we are not even able to uphold our own:

> And the little ones that you said would be taken captive, your children who do not yet know good from bad—they will enter the land. I will give it to them and they will take possession of it.[115]

We are often encouraged to downplay the eternal effects of our decisions in our lives. However, one day the bill will come due, and it will need to be paid. Though it has already been paid for on the cross, to those who despise the Benefactor, the price will be their lives.

In all honesty, it is quite difficult to make excuses for an omniscient and omnipresent God who hears even our quietest murmurs. We deceive people around us, and at times deceive ourselves. We strive to believe our own lies, living in a world of illusion and falsehood. God, however, not only sees and hears all things, but also

---

[115] Deuteronomy 1:39

searches our hearts. He knows our deepest desires, and as such, is just in all His verdicts. [116]

Despite the horrific appearance, we may have in His eyes, God does not reject us, but is always ready to receive us and shower us with His grace.[117] Our best response to His love for us is the humble recognition of our sinful condition. Only when we are transparent with Him and sincere in our relationship can we be healed and perfected from the deformities caused by sin. When we yield ourselves by faith to His grace, we are covered by the blood of Christ; and thus, being hid in Him, His beauty is revealed in us. Only when the Son is seen in us, do we become attractive in the Father's eyes. For this is the power of the wonderful work that Christ accomplished on that cross, capable of transforming sinners like us into beloved children of the Most High.[118]

And despite Israel's rebellion, the Lord continued to work on His plans. Even amidst so much sin and death, He still showed signs of His grace. One such sign was choosing to spare those of 20 years and younger, so that, in the future, they might receive the inheritance promised to their parents:

> Because they have not followed me wholeheartedly, not one of those who were twenty years old or more when they came up out of Egypt will see the land I

---

[116] Luke 12:2; Romans 2:16; 1 Corinthians 4:5; Hebrews 4:13, etc.
[117] Psalm 34:18, 51:17
[118] Isaiah 53:4-7; Luke 4:18-19

promised on oath to Abraham, Isaac and Jacob— not one except Caleb son of Jephunneh the Kenizzite and Joshua son of Nun, for they followed the Lord wholeheartedly.' The Lord's anger burned against Israel, and he made them wander in the wilderness forty years, until the whole generation of those who had done evil in his sight was gone.[119]

Even so, the consequences for their rebellion were severe, and the Israelites would have to spend all that time in the desert reflecting on their disobedience. As each funeral took place, it is not difficult to imagine that they would have been reminded that this person had died without experiencing the blessings of the Promised Land due to their lack of trust in the Lord. And though they must have been saddened by this, perhaps they looked onto their children with hope, knowing one day they would be the ones to finally taste the goodness of God in the land promised to Abraham.

While the fear of that rebellious generation had not been enough to derail God's plans, that their children would be blessed despite their parents' rebellion clearly reveals God's righteousness and loving character. Though punishing the guilty (but not before offering them countless opportunities to repent), God also spared the innocent, offering them life and a right to enter the new land. In doing so, not only did God redeem that unbelieving generation from their own mistakes, but also

---

[119] Numbers 32:11-13, cf. 14:29

reaffirmed His eternal purpose of redemption for humanity. For it would be from this people, around 1,400 years later, that the Saviour of mankind would appear.

As we try to understand our confusing world, we can be confident in the promise that God will soon restore creation in its entirety. He will not fail to give us the new heavens and the new earth, where we will enjoy perfect justice in every conceivable way. This justice, be it moral, social, emotional, material, or spiritual, will be made, sustained, and approved by Him.[120] The author Phillip Yancey compellingly invites us to trust in God's promise:

> We can trust God even when all the evidence seems to be against us. We can believe that He controls the universe and promises that one day, there will be a much better world, a world where there will be no pain, evil or anguish.[121]

Next, we see how the Lord deals with the just, when He does not forget about Caleb and Joshua:

> No one who has treated me with contempt will ever see it. But because my servant Caleb has a different spirit and follows me wholeheartedly, I will bring him into the land he went to, and his descendants will inherit it. [...] Not one of you will enter the land [...],

---

[120] Isaiah 32:15-18, 65:17; Matthew 25:34; Romans 8:21; 2 Peter 3:13; Revelations 21:1-8

[121] Free translation of Philip Yancey, When Life Hurts, United Press, 2003, p. 26

except Caleb son of Jephunneh and Joshua son of Nun.[122]

Earnestly analysing this episode of the spies exploring the land and subsequent rebellion, one can imagine how difficult it must have been for Caleb and Joshua to remain faithful to both God and Moses in the face of such staunch opposition. It was only the two of them against ten others, who were also leaders in their respective tribes. Not only were they refuting the false report of the other leaders, but also had to face the people themselves, who were now all but ready to give up the whole enterprise.

It does not take much effort to assume the two trembled in fear when the people began picking up rocks to stone them. Caleb and Joshua had been accused, tried, and sentenced to death before the congregation without Aaron or Moses being able to defend them. It was only the Lord's intervention that brought that chaotic and unfortunate scene to an end.[123] Even then, when faced with the disapproval of almost an entire nation, these two men kept a different spirit, deciding to swim against the current. Their faith nearly cost them not just their leadership, but also their lives. The example of integrity of Caleb and Joshua was not in vain, for the Lord noticed and preserved them.

---

[122] Numbers 14:23-24, 29-30
[123] Numbers 14:10

The Bible says that God knows those who love Him. It is one thing for you to know God, but it is another entirely for God to know you. On that final day, He will turn His divine countenance to you and recognize you. He will know your name not simply because He is God and knows all things, but because He knows how much you loved Him.

Thirty-eight years later, the new generation returned to Canaan. Caleb and Joshua, both now eighty years old, returned with them. After Moses, they were the oldest people in all of Israel, with the rest being the children and people up to twenty years of age at the time of the rebellion. Now, so many years later, they finally stood together before the land, lining up to possess it.

Moses, now in his final days, turns to this new generation and retells the story of how God had delivered their people out of Egypt. He reiterates God's laws, reminding them of their parents' rebellion, and emphasizes how great a privilege the Lord was granting them.

This final speech by Moses, delivered on the plains of Moab, is recorded in the book of Deuteronomy, the fifth book of the Bible. Its title comes from the Hebrew word, דְּבָרִים, *Devārim*, meaning "words spoken (by Moses)"[124], and well represents the intentions behind its contents. In this sense, Deuteronomy can be seen as Moses' final testament or orientation to the people for the transition period to come.

It is satisfying to see that, in his final words, Moses includes a passage mentioned by God many years before, during the days of the rebellion. He declares that Caleb and his descendants would possess the land he had trodden on in his expedition with the other spies, the land called Hebron.[125]

Using a little imagination, we can see the younger Caleb attempting to calm the people, urging them to take courage and fight for the land. Then, we see the people interrupting his speech in a great uproar, taking him, and attempting to kill him. Next, we see the Lord doing the interrupting, by stopping the people and sparing Caleb from being stoned. What follows is an almost forty-year hiatus of wandering through the desert, at the end of which Caleb returns to the same spot.

---

[124] Observe how Deuteronomy begins in 1:1 with the phrase "These are the words spoken by Moses."
[125] Deuteronomy 1:36

Facing Hebron once again, Caleb rejoices in the hope of finally possessing the land he had been dreaming of for so long. Having finally passed the time since their failed attempt to possess the land, Moses leads the people back through the desert to the gates of Canaan. Moses was not to enter the land himself, as the time for his final departure had come. Before dying, Moses went up to Mount Nebo, from where God showed him the land where Israel would finally dwell.[126] After this, "Moses, the servant of the LORD, died there in Moab."[127]

It is no wonder "the Israelites mourned for Moses [...] for thirty days"[128] afterwards, as, without a doubt, he is one of the most important figures in Scripture. His name alone is mentioned about eight hundred times by biblical authors. From his birth as a slave in Egypt, to being adopted by Pharaoh's daughter, then turning into a fugitive in the desert for forty years, and finally becoming a deliverer to his people, the story of Moses is marked by God's sovereignty.

Now under Joshua's leadership, Israel begins its invasion of Canaan, gradually taking possession of the land. Five years later, after a series of initial attacks, Caleb prepares to fight for Hebron, forty-five years after the Israelites' initial revolt. His opening speech, recorded in Numbers 13:30, appears as a continuation of earlier

---

[126] Deuteronomy 34:1-4
[127] Deuteronomy 34:5
[128] Deuteronomy 34:8

speeches, resumed after a long break. It is as if for Caleb these forty-five years had only been a "parenthesis" in life.

It is difficult to find joy amidst persecution and rejection for Jesus' sake. However, that is precisely what is asked of us. For a reward awaits those whose names are mocked by men and honoured by Christ.

Caleb's vigor and eagerness are so great that one would think he had never even been stopped in the first place. He turns to Joshua and reminds him that Hebron was the Lord's promise to him. His enthusiasm made that long hiatus seem like the blink of an eye, as is always the case when hope is rewarded. Caleb resumes his speech in Joshua 14:6 with the same faith and confidence that had captured God's attention many years before. And now, the eighty-five-year-old and not-so-young Caleb says he is ready and willing to finally conquer his share of the land, as promised by God:[129]

---

[129] Numbers 14:24; Deuteronomy 1:36; Joshua 14:12

"Now then, just as the Lord promised, he has kept me alive for forty-five years since the time he said this to Moses, while Israel moved about in the wilderness. So here I am today, eighty-five years old! I am still as strong today as the day Moses sent me out; I'm just as vigorous to go out to battle now as I was then. Now give me this hill country that the Lord promised me that day. You yourself heard then that the Anakites were there, and their cities were large and fortified, but, the Lord helping me, I will drive them out just as he said." Then Joshua blessed Caleb son of Jephunneh and gave him Hebron as his inheritance. [130]

Caleb knew Hebron's dangers and wonders, as he had walked through it during his mission with the spies. He also knew of Hebron's history and connection with Abraham the patriarch. But regardless of the land's significance, riches, or hazards, the main reason Caleb wanted it so much was the simple fact that God had promised it to him. This is how Hebron came to belong to the descendants of "Caleb son of Jephunneh the Kenizzite [...] because he followed the Lord, the God of Israel, wholeheartedly. [...] Then the land had rest from war."[131]

Naturally, Joshua was also blessed by God in the entire process. He was chosen as the new leader of Israel, succeeding Moses in this extraordinary mission. The

---

[130] Joshua 14:10-13
[131] Joshua 14:14-15

Lord had instructed Moses to train Joshua as his helper and to encourage him during all those years of wandering. It was God himself who told Moses that Joshua would be the one to claim the inheritance for Israel.[132] With Moses gone, it fell on him the honor and responsibility of leading this new generation of Israelites in the conquest of Canaan. For the great challenge ahead of them, the Lord blessed Joshua with enough courage, allowing him to continue God's wonderful plan for the redemption of humanity.

In a way, Joshua redeemed Israel from the wandering in the wilderness, finally giving them rest after a long and turbulent journey. For this reason, Joshua is held by biblical scholars as another type of Christ in the Old Testament, for by saving his people from exile in the desert, Joshua did something similar to what Jesus would do many years later. What Jesus did definitively for us through His death and resurrection, Joshua did provisionally for the people of Israel, and on a much smaller scale.

The author of the book of Hebrews mentions Joshua as a typification of the work of Christ.[133] In fact, the names of both in Hebrew are written the same. Both Jesus and Joshua are written as יהושוע, *Yehōshua*, or *Yeshūa*, meaning "the Lord saves" or "the Lord is salvation". The New Testament, written in Greek,

---

[132] Deuteronomy 1:38
[133] Hebrews 4:8-11

brought the transliteration of the name Yeshua into Ἰησοῦς, *Iēsoûs*, and then later, into Latin as Jesus.

Have your eyes of faith been opened yet? Can you see the reward that God has for you? It is invaluable, incomparable, and worthwhile. Now is not the time to give up: take courage!

The conquest of Canaan was neither easy, nor did it happen overnight. Taking possession of the Promised Land took faith and courage to obey God and to carry out His plan. The biblical text recounts how that land had many enemies to be expelled. Then, after defeating those enemies, the Hebrews still needed to prepare the land for permanent settlement. There were many struggles, and they would need to make great effort so they could finally enjoy the land.

Some of the tribes of Israel were unable to fully appropriate the land allocated to them, having to live with other peoples for many years. The book of Judges tells us that the tribe of Benjamin was unable to get rid of the Jebusites living in Jerusalem and they had to live side by side for many years. There are so many other examples like this, such as the tribes of Manasseh, Ephraim,

Zebulun, Asher, and Naphtali who never managed to expel the people who lived in their land before the invasion. Asher, for example, settled with the Canaanites, as they could not get rid of them.[134] Even King David, nearly four hundred years later, still had to contend with many of these enemies. Perhaps the best-known example of this is David's expulsion of the Jebusites from the city he would eventually name Jerusalem.[135]

For this reason, from the very beginning of Joshua's leadership, the Lord Himself instructed him to guide the people in the new land with courage, while urging him not to deviate from His Word. These two things – His Word and our courage – needed to go together. Courage to lead under God's Word is the only option, especially when we speak the truth that sets people free, and realize there may be "wild wolves" who "will come in among you", and that there may also be men "from among your own selves" who will try to lead Christians away from the truth (Acts 20:29-30). Courage, as we know, comes from believing that something is so precious that it's worth fighting for. We will always act according to what we believe.

In dividing the land amongst the tribes of Israel, Joshua made a final appeal to his brothers. He knew how their ancestors had been rebellious against the Lord and how this new generation was in danger of falling into the same error as their parents. And now he would have the

---

[134] For more on the conquest of Canaan, see Joshua 11-17, Judges 1.
[135] 2 Samuel 5:6-7

task of shepherding this people, as Moses had done before him.

Fear the Lord and serve Him with all faithfulness. Now, make your choice! But as for me and my house, we will serve the Lord.

This new generation was to be the recipient of the promise made to Abraham hundreds of years earlier. It would take a heart of integrity, one that does not deviate from the laws of the Lord and remains faithful in all circumstances. Enabled by his experiences, and with the authority God had given him, Joshua then challenges the people before him:

> Throw away the gods your ancestors worshiped beyond the Euphrates River and in Egypt, and serve the Lord. But if serving the Lord seems undesirable to you, then choose for yourselves this day whom you will serve, whether the gods your ancestors served beyond the Euphrates, or the gods of the Amorites, in whose land you are living. But as for me and my household, we will serve the Lord.[136]

---

[136] Joshua 24:14-15

Though not to blame for the rebellion of the other spies, Caleb and Joshua suffered with the people during that lengthy period of waiting. However, they were willing to persevere. Encouraged by God, they looked forward to the fulfilment of His promise. And that same hope must be in the hearts of all those who wait for the Day of the Lord:

> For the grace of God has appeared that offers salvation to all people. It teaches us to say "No" to ungodliness and worldly passions, and to live self-controlled, upright and godly lives in this present age, *while we wait for the blessed hope—the appearing of the glory of our great God and Savior, Jesus Christ,* who gave himself for us to redeem us from all wickedness and to purify for himself a people that are his very own, eager to do what is good.[137]

---

[137] Titus 2:11-14

05 Conclusion: Promise Made Promise Kept

Without shame and without doubt you may eat the Flesh and drink the Blood if you are desirous of true life.
Gregory of Nazianzus

Never be afraid to trust an unknown future to a known God.
Corrie ten Boom

Consecrate yourselves, for tomorrow the Lord will do amazing things among you.
Joshua 3:5

Mario Quintana, the Brazilian "poet of simple things", writes plainly yet powerfully about the truth of life:

> Life is like schoolwork we bring to do at home. When you look, it's already 6 o'clock… You look again, and it's already Friday… You look one more time, and it's already been 60 years… And now, it's far too late to fail… If they'd given me just one more day—just one more opportunity, I wouldn't even look at the clock; I would always, always just look straight ahead.[138]

The Lord had pledged His name by signing the solemn declaration that He would fulfill the promise made to Abraham and give the land to the Israelites: "I will bring you to the land I swore with uplifted hand to give to Abraham, to Isaac and to Jacob. I will give it to you as a possession – *I am the LORD*".[139] It can't get any better than this. Even at the beginning of the journey, when the Israelites at the Red Sea were afraid of Pharaoh, the Lord said to them, "Fear not, stand still and see the salvation of God." All the way through, He showed Himself faithful. As Spurgeon said, whenever "we observe the Scriptures, we perceive that 'Fear nots' are scattered throughout the Bible as the stars are sprinkled over the whole of the sky".[140] Still, the Israelites did not trust in the Lord, and after testing the Lord so much, it was too late for them.

---

[138] Free translation of Mario Quintana, Esconderijos do Tempo, Ed Objetiva, 2013, p. 38

[139] Exodus 6:8

[140] spurgeon.org/resource-library/sermons/fear-not, March 9, 1880

Rare are the moments when we can recover lost opportunity. The Israelites, having heard the Lord's sentence for their rebellion, desperately tried to fix the situation themselves. They decided to enter Canaan from the south, where the Amalekites and Canaanites lived. But God had forbidden them to do so, and Moses warned them:

> Why are you disobeying the Lord's command? This will not succeed! Do not go up, because the Lord is not with you. You will be defeated by your enemies, for the Amalekites and the Canaanites will face you there. Because you have turned away from the Lord, he will not be with you, and you will fall by the sword.[141]

As predicted, their assault was a complete disaster, and they were eventually defeated at Horma. Though we can always count on God's grace, some things are simply irrecoverable. Thus, the Bible invites us to seize every opportunity that arises[142], as they are a gift from God.

Many years later, the apostle Paul makes a reference to this remarkable and dramatic event as he writes to the church in Corinth. The Corinthians had been privileged with many blessings but were similarly living on the verge of disaster and loss of divine favor. They had forgotten the importance of living under the sign of the Cross and were instead showing signs of immorality and

---

[141] Numbers 14:41-43
[142] Ephesians 5:16

disobedience. Paul then uses the image of Israel's rebellion as an illustration to warn them of their own arrogance, as the many blessings and privileges we receive from God cannot be used as a free pass or as an excuse for sin.

Certainly, that rebellious generation of Israel had been greatly privileged by the Lord. He had freed them from slavery in Egypt, led them by His *mighty hand*[143] through the desert, and safely brought them to the lands of Canaan; day and night had the Lord personally guided them. Paul reminds his readers in Corinth of how the Israelites had passed through the waters of the Red Sea, just as we have passed through the waters of our baptism in Christ. Moreover, God had also provided the Israelites with daily meals of food and water; water from the Rock, which was Christ.[144]

This had been provided to the contemporaries of Moses, Joshua, and Caleb solely by the grace of God. Repeatedly, we see glimpses of just how much they had been blessed, all the while witnessing events never lived through before or since. This makes it one of the most defining moments both in the history of Israel and in the biblical narrative. Most shocking is Paul's assertion that those wonderful privileges and signs did not seem to have the necessary impact on people to motivate them to remain faithful in the day of temptation. They chose to believe the promises offered by fear (that they would be

---

[143] Exodus 13:16
[144] 1 Corinthians 10:1-4

destroyed) rather than trusting that God would give them the land. And naturally, the Lord wasn't pleased with them.[145]

Psalm 78, which tells the story of Israel from Moses to David, points to this contrast between the goodness of God and the unfaithfulness of men. Poetically, the Psalmist insists, verse after verse, on how God brought the people out of captivity, personally leading them, only for Israel to reject Him:

> But he brought his people out like a flock; he led them like sheep through the wilderness. He guided them safely, so they were unafraid; but the sea engulfed their enemies. And so he brought them to the border of his holy land, to the hill country his right hand had taken. [...] But they put God to the test and rebelled against the Most High; they did not keep his statutes.[146]

Paul continues his letter to the Corinthians by warning them that "these things occurred as examples *to keep us from setting our hearts on evil things as they did.*"[147] It was Paul's fear that just as the Israelites ended up perishing in the desert, so too would the church in Corinth. He feared they might be disqualified in the eyes of God, certainly a tragedy. If the church did not realize the gravity of their arrogance and pride, they would be in the same danger as

---

[145] 1 Corinthians 10:5
[146] Psalm 78:52-54, 56
[147] 1 Corinthians 10:6

the Israelites, who wasted their lives wandering in the wilderness for forty years, becoming useless to the Kingdom.

Unfortunately, there will always be those who abuse their privileges, becoming conceited, proud, and fearful. They become the focus of their own lives, like the rebellious Israelites, who act only to their own benefit. They live in search of someone who can spy out, or check out the land on their behalf; someone who can show them whether the next chapters of their lives will be safe and profitable, someone, such as guides, coaches, prophets, etc. In such cases, the expansion of God's Kingdom really is out of the question. They spend their days wandering, one after the other, until death arrives, finally closing the cycle of yet another useless life.

The past can teach us many things, with even previous failures being excellent educators. But now, with these lessons learned, we need to look forward. God wants us to walk by faith at all times— at all times.

So, where did the Israelites go wrong? Paul interrupts the story to explain that those people had desired evil things in their hearts, and now he hopes we will not do the same. They lost their privilege of entering the Promised Land because they had desired things contrary to what God had established. They were disqualified because they failed in their devotion to God.

In 1 Corinthians 10:7-10, we read in more detail what sort of *evil things* the Israelites were doing. "Do not be idolaters, as some of them were", says the text, with Psalm 78:58 also mentioning this same idolatry. Similarly, this was happening at the church in Corinth. They had continued to participate in idolatrous feasts, eating and drinking with pagan worshippers, while at the same time, wanting to sit at the Communion table. They were associating themselves with two things that Paul warned were contradictory:

> But the sacrifices of pagans are offered to demons, not to God, and I do not want you to be participants with demons. You cannot drink the cup of the Lord and the cup of demons too; you cannot have a part in both the Lord's table and the table of demons.[148]

Idolatrous feasts are incompatible with a friendship with God, and we see several instances of this in the Old Testament. One such episode sees the Israelites eating, drinking, and offering sacrifices in worship of a golden calf.[149]

---

[148] 1 Corinthians 10:20-21
[149] Exodus 32:1-4

Another evil act mentioned by Paul was their involvement in some form of sexual immorality: "We should not commit sexual immorality, as some of them did", says the apostle.[150] In Exodus 32:6, we see the Israelites participating in these types of feasts, implying involvement in some kind of orgy, as was common with certain types of idol worship. Hence, Paul urges the church in Corinth not to provoke the Lord like those in the past. Just as the Lord Jesus Himself said, "Do not put the Lord your God to the test."[151]

We should not allow the *evil things* mentioned by Paul to find room in our hearts, thus turning into idols in our eyes. Anything can become an idol or a deity when we bow down to it and allow ourselves to be under its control. Therefore, we must be careful as to not push the limits of what is permissible, and in turn, test the Lord, as we would risk receiving the same punishment as that unfaithful generation of Israel.

Finally, Paul mentions a third evil act common among the Israelites. This was the sin of grumbling or murmuring, already discussed at length in this book. Paul insists that this grumbling is an offensive posture towards God, that of one who is constantly complaining against Him. The consequence of such attitude was the destruction of those people: "And do not grumble, as

---

[150] 1 Corinthians 10:8; cf. Numbers 25:1-8
[151] Matthew 4:7

some of them did—and were killed by the destroying angel."[152]

Sin is always knocking at our door. If you give it the opportunity, it will insist, until the day it manages to enter. Then, it will sit on the throne of your heart and take charge of your life. It might feel strange at first, and you might even want to fight against it, but sure enough, little by little, it will start to feel normal. Jesus also knocks at the door of our heart, and there will not be enough room for both.

Overall, it is a heavy list that Paul presents. The people of Israel committed these transgressions all along their pilgrimage, from their departure in Egypt to their arrival in the Promised Land. They engaged in idolatry, immorality, and murmuring, all acts contrary to the will of God. Their willingness to sin was a constant test of the Lord's patience. Every time they crossed the line between holiness and sin, their conscience was seared, to the point

---

[152] 1 Corinthians 10:10

of sin becoming normal and commonplace. Eventually, it became their way of life.

Now, with their minds dulled by the routine practice of sin, Israel lost their fear of the Lord—the only fear they should have kept.[153] Gradually, Israel distanced itself from God and let their relationship grow cold. And when time finally came to be obedient and courageous, the people were afraid; not of God, but of the false promises fear offered them. In their doubt-infested hearts, there was no more room to trust God.

The story of the Israelites has practical implications for us. Paul understands the seriousness of their mistakes and warns us not to run the same risk of arrogance that led to their fall:

> These things happened to them as examples and were written down as warnings for us, on whom the culmination of the ages has come. So, if you think you are standing firm, be careful that you don't fall![154]

Likewise, we have been blessed with many privileges, and must remain watchful. We must always be vigilant lest we fall and become useless in the Kingdom of God. This is not easy as we live in a world surrounded by an attractive and cunning system, one designed and well prepared to subtly seduce us. We cannot forget that we ourselves are also marred by sin, and as such, have a

---

[153] Psalm 25:12-14; Psalm 128; Proverbs 9:10; Matthew 10:28
[154] 1 Corinthians 10:11-12

natural tendency[155] to be seduced. We are always at risk of being swallowed up by this system, or at least to be imprinted by it and take its values and practices for ourselves.

Thankfully, God's providence is sufficient to help us through these struggles. We need to be alert, but not afraid. Though powerful, neither the Devil nor the systems he uses against us are stronger than the Spirit that dwells within us.[156] It is, then, within this context of the history of Israel that Paul fills us with the hope needed to succeed in the day of struggle:

> No temptation has overtaken you except what is common to mankind. And God is faithful; he will not let you be tempted beyond what you can bear. But when you are tempted, he will also provide a way out so that you can endure it.[157]

None of the tests or temptations we must pass through will be beyond what we can bear. This means struggles can be faced and defeated. They will be within human limits and will not be anything special, supernatural or beyond our powers. Paul reminds us of God's faithfulness, and He will not let us down by putting us in battles greater than we can manage. He will never

---

[155] Hosea 11:7
[156] 1 John 4:4
[157] 1 Corinthians 10:13

allow that limit to be crossed. Additionally, He Himself will always be there to help us through all struggles.

When Paul states that there is no temptation that has come upon us except for what is human, he uses the Greek word ἀνθρώπινος, anthrópinos, to mean that it is something typical or strictly human. In other words, it is not something supernatural or superhuman that will come upon us, but rather something bearable for human beings. Ultimately, these things cannot dominate us, as God, in His faithfulness, will not allow us to be tempted beyond what we can overcome.

And this was the same plan the Lord had for the people of Israel in the deserts of Kadesh-Barnea. He knew the enemies of that land and He knew the challenges His children would have to face to conquer it. Nothing in that process was a surprise for God. He was aware of the strengths and abilities of those involved and was certainly not leading His own people into a trap. On the contrary! Paul firmly declares: *God is faithful.* As you might remember, just before the spies left on their fateful mission, God reminded them that this was "the land I am giving to the Israelites."[158] They most certainly could face those giants, as the land was already theirs.

We all go through times of fear in life, but the question is how we react to it. The biblical answer to this is found in the level of depth in our relationship with God. The

---

[158] Numbers 13:1

more we love Him, the less we will fear. The prophet Isaiah, for example, warns us against paranoia by advising us not to be like those who are always afraid someone is conspiring against them: "Do not fear what they fear, nor worry as they do." He continues by saying that if our attention needs to be focused on something or someone, then let it be on God: "Fear the Holy One of Israel," he says.[159] A certain awe or reverence for the Lord must take root in our hearts so that it may drive out the fears of our real or imagined conspiracies.

The apostle John declares that only when we remain in a real love relationship with God, we will be safe to live and die. God is love, he says, and we must invest in that love until we are enveloped and overshadowed by it. When we are surrounded by God's love, it takes control of our lives and bestows us with peace and security. This love relationship then dispels all the exaggerated worries of our minds, be them about tomorrow or the Day of Judgement.[160]

This love cannot be superficial, fleeting, or otherwise go unnurtured. It needs to grow and mature, taking over the spaces in our hearts, so that faith in fear will never have enough room. Therefore, when we finally come to understand the unmerited privilege of being loved by God, we are compelled to reciprocate it.[161] And when this

---

[159] Isaiah 8:11-13
[160] 1 John 4:16-19
[161] 2 Corinthians 5:14

love is cultivated and strengthened, it transforms us, giving us freedom from the bonds of fear and guilt.

In God, everything is great. His love, His power, His plans. Nothing is small or insignificant. This includes the paths He has laid out for each one of us. Though we may not fully understand it now, it will all be made clear when we enter through the eternal gates. Until then, it is only by faith that we can see this heavenly vision.

Likewise, just as the Lord had assured the people He would bless them in that new land, Paul says that God has *already* blessed us in the heavenly realms.[162] I will say it again: He has *already* blessed us. The understanding of this truth must then be transformed into faith and is sufficient to face any struggle. Not only will the Promised Land make up for any heartache we experience along the way, but the confidence that one day we will finally possess it

---

[162] Ephesians 1:3

should transform the way we live our lives, whether in joy or in sadness.[163]

Conversely, the absence of faith cripples us, and makes us languish in apprehensive, anxious, and trivial lives. Like the Israelites, we would simply spend our time walking through the desert, waiting for death to arrive. Those who live like this and are not yet established in God's love require constant motivation, living as if the desert were their permanent home.

In addition to the fear of facing the giants of the Promised Land, the Israelites also had to rely on God for their daily provisions. This eventually led to them simply preferring to die in the desert, their easiest and most convenient option. In a way, the faithful distribution of sustenance then became an invitation for them to accommodate themselves to their wanderings. What should have been a short transition phase between slavery and full freedom became desired as permanent. Thus, they got stuck in their nomadic lifestyle.

The initial belief of striving to enter into rest[164] was slowly abandoned, and the momentum gained from leaving slavery was lost entirely. This was replaced by their new normal, a state of contentment with mediocrity. Contentment with abundance is not synonymous with

---

163 Romans 8:18
164 Hebrews 4:10-11

earthly prosperity, but rather, with spiritual prosperity.[165] It is about letting heaven fill our hearts, and letting it guide us *across* the desert towards itself. C.S. Lewis writes on how we became too fond of the desert, ignorant of another and far better offering:

> We are half-hearted creatures, fooling about with drink and sex and ambition when infinite joy is offered us, like an ignorant child who wants to go on making mud pies in a slum because he cannot imagine what is meant by the offer of a holiday at the sea. We are far too easily pleased.[166]

We are often tempted to cling to our work, pastimes, pleasures, and dreams. The desert, made to be crossed, has become an attractive destination, swaying our mood away from decisively declaring that we prefer to enter God's rest. The Christian must learn how to walk that fine line— that dilemma—between living in this land while dreaming of another. It is only then that we can make the best use of our limited time crossing this desert. And as for Paul, he found his answer in his love for Christ:

> For to me, to live is Christ and to die is gain. If I am to go on living in the body, this will mean fruitful labor for me. Yet what shall I choose? I do not know! I am torn between the two: I desire to depart and be with Christ, which is better by far.[167]

---

165 3 John 2

166C.S. Lewis, The Weight of Glory, HarperCollins, 1980, p. 26

167 Philippians 1:21-23

Those who have already come out of the bondage of sin and are now going through the nomadic and transient phase of this earth should know that this is not the end. Quite the opposite. The blessings and struggles we experience here on earth point to the incomparable offer of the full freedom that will soon follow - like Abraham, the great patriarch and father of faith, who lived in temporary tents while awaiting "the city with foundations, whose architect and builder is God." He "made his home in the promised land like a stranger in a foreign country" and recognized that he and his family were only "foreigners and strangers on earth." He was just passing through, "seeking a country of their own."[168]

I have been to places where I really felt like a foreigner. But despite the constant reminder that this was not my land, I could still enjoy some of its marvels. Other times, however, I was also reminded I had a family and a home elsewhere, whom I missed. It is the same with heaven and earth.

---

[168] Hebrews 11:9-10, 13-14

We cannot waste our lives fruitlessly wandering in the desert chasing after the wind.[169] The understanding that we are heirs of God's blessings should propel us to be productive in this crossing and not lazily rely on miracles. We should be anticipating, so to speak, the samples of heaven here on earth.

These heavenly manifestations in our lives can serve as small oases, giving much needed respite in an otherwise arid landscape. Of course, these should only serve as small rest stops that ultimately point to that eternal rest. Living for the Kingdom should not be characterized by the arid desert, but by the fertile plains in between, a place where we can grow bountiful fruit for the glory of God. Jesus said that when we are connected to Him, we can produce much, regardless of location or circumstance: "If you remain in me and I in you, you will bear much fruit."[170]

So, with all the privileges we have received along the journey, we must be careful not to allow faith in fear to make us walk in circles and to prevent us from reaching the Promised Land. As we have seen, it can be a subtle agent, presenting us with obstacles to discourage us, while seemingly offering us benefits and inviting us to settle down. God does not want us to be timid in using the gifts He has bestowed on us, but rather bold, loving, and temperate, and to respond to His calling for us.[171] In other

---

[169] Ecclesiastes 2:17
[170] John 15:1-5
[171] 2 Timothy 1:6-9

words, these gifts should be put into use and acted upon without delay.

Fear, together with self-indulgence and conceit, cause us to look inward, leading to selfishness and pride. As these tendencies grow inside us, we become our only focus, and begin to lose sight of everything else. Inversely, faith in God leads us to gaze heavenward, switching our focus to the Lord and what He can do in and through us. This leads to an altruistic life, whose sole purpose is to live for the sake of the Kingdom.

When the children of that rebellious generation finally returned to the gates of Canaan after their long desert pilgrimage (in Joshua 1:1-9), Moses stood up to encourage them one last time. He instructed them to support Joshua as their new leader and to take courage, as much of it would still be needed in the days ahead. God personally called upon Joshua to instruct him and to give him His assurance. I like how Eugene Peterson captures this moment in history in his *The Message* translation:

> After the death of Moses, the servant of God, God spoke to Joshua, Moses' assistant: "Moses my servant is dead. Get going. Cross this Jordan River, you and all the people. Cross to the country I'm giving to the People of Israel. I'm giving you every square inch of the land you set your foot on—just as I promised Moses. From the wilderness and this Lebanon east to the Great River, the Euphrates River—all the Hittite country—and then west to the Great Sea. It's all yours.

All your life, no one will be able to hold out against you. In the same way I was with Moses, I'll be with you. I won't give up on you; I won't leave you. Strength! Courage! You are going to lead this people to inherit the land that I promised to give their ancestors. Give it everything you have, heart and soul. Make sure you carry out The Revelation that Moses commanded you, every bit of it. Don't get off track, either left or right, so as to make sure you get to where you're going. And don't for a minute let this Book of The Revelation be out of mind. Ponder and meditate on it day and night, making sure you practice everything written in it. Then you'll get where you're going; then you'll succeed. Haven't I commanded you? Strength! Courage! Don't be timid; don't get discouraged. God, your God, is with you every step you take.

Often are the times when we, under pressure, think about giving up, be it on a project, a relationship or even on life itself. "There are times when Satan whispers, 'God will leave you. God will forsake you. He has done all this for you, and yet he will leave you.' Ah, but He never will, for His faithfulness never fails".[172] We need to be aware that no enemy can steal our true treasure—that is, our salvation. Everything else is fleeting, having no guarantees that we will keep it forever. Still, we can always look forward to God's daily provisions, remembering the greatest provision of all was already made and signed with His irrevocable guarantee on the cross.

---

[172] C.H. Spurgeon. spurgeon.org/resource-library/sermons/fear-not

> *No promise of God ever fails. All are true and will faithfully be fulfilled. The Bible reminds us of this through Jesus' sacrifice on the cross, a covenant signed in blood—His blood. Despite the high price, this offer was provided to us free of charge, and all that is required of us is to have faith.*

We need to keep in mind that the same Jesus who proved His love for us on the cross will always be in the presence of God advocating for us: we are not alone. Could anything or anyone make Him stop loving us? Paul was absolutely convinced that nothing—not life, not death, not angels or demons, not the present nor the future, neither heights nor depths; absolutely nothing could come between us and the love of God. A love, moreover, personally guaranteed to us by His son, Jesus Christ.[173]

Therefore, we should not despise this truth and these promises. We should consider with great attention the example of the Israelites turning their backs on God after being rescued from slavery. We are in the middle of the

---

[173] Romans 8:35-39

crossing, of the conquest, with our eyes turned towards the Promised Land. The Bible says that it will not be much longer and that our Lord is already on His way. He may appear to us at any moment. When He does finally come, we will wake up to a joy never to be taken away.[174] This joy will be incomparably superior, surpassing any pain or suffering we have experienced on this earth.

For now, we continue our walk through the desert, relying on God's provisions and knowing that this is the time to persevere, to insist, to believe. We cannot turn our backs now. Believe, and be saved:

> So do not throw away your confidence; it will be richly rewarded. You need to persevere so that when you have done the will of God, you will receive what he has promised. For, "In just a little while, he who is coming will come and will not delay." And, "But my righteous one will live by faith. And I take no pleasure in the one who shrinks back."[175]

When besieged with fear, we must remember God's love for us, asking ourselves if we really have no reason to have confidence in His care. It is so we can challenge ourselves to wait on God.: "Why, my soul, are you downcast?"[176]

---

[174] John 16:22
[175] Hebrews 10:35-39
[176] Psalm 42:5

But we do not belong to those who shrink back and are destroyed, but to those who have faith and are saved.

Luke 12:32, Jesus challenges us to trust in the God who has promised us eternal life: "Fear not, little flock, for it is your Father's good pleasure to give you the kingdom". He urges us not to fear and gives us three good reasons why. In this short verse, our Master offers us a threefold descriptive image of our God. First, He calls us *little flock*, an obvious allusion to His shepherding over us. We have a Shepherd who gave His life to save His flock. Second, He specifically calls God *our Father*. We are not orphaned, forgotten, and we do not need to fear the temporary struggles during the journey: "Your heavenly Father knows what you need". Our God understands our desires. Finally, the third image is that of the King. God will share the *kingdom* with us. Even if we don't have everything here in this world, we are heirs to a superior and eternal Kingdom. Be of good cheer about this.

Yes, our inheritance is yet to come. What a joy to know that we are accompanied on this journey by the Shepherd, the Father and the King. The Father loves us. The Shepherd guides us and the King waits for us with the promise to provide the way until we get Home.

Take your Bible and let the Lord's promises calm your heart. Whatever level of despair and fear you find yourself in, remember that you can always come back to God's promises. In your relationship with Him, you can rest safely in His faithfulness and His power, knowing He will keep you. And so, without turning back, you will be able to "run with perseverance the race marked out for us, fixing our eyes on Jesus, the pioneer and perfecter of faith."[177]

Do not be surprised at the many trials that we will face throughout our lives.[178] Look at the cross! It is the proof that the Lord's promises will be fulfilled. As Christians, we must remember that God is never taken aback or found in a panic. Being in perfect peace, He loves us with His incomparable strength.[179] We can see from Scripture and even in experiences throughout our lives that God is not indifferent to us. He is not distant or aloof, but "near to all who call on Him."[180]

Amid the chaos and panic of life, we can express our faith to others, letting it infect those we love with the same peace and confidence that assures us. Our faith is built upon the Lord Most High, the Holy One, who does not panic, but is always calm and in control of history: "I will remain quiet and will look on from my dwelling place, like

---

[177] Hebrews 12:1-2
[178] James 1:2
[179] Ephesians 1:19
[180] Psalm 145:18

shimmering heat in the sunshine, like a cloud of dew in the heat of harvest."[181]

Jesus wants our relationship with Him to bring us peace. And if the realities of life tell us that "in this world you will have trouble", Jesus tells us to take courage, for He has "overcome the world."[182]

Like an athlete training for a race, so too does faith require daily practice. Similarly, just as they must eat certain foods while abstaining from others, so too do we need to do or abstain from certain things by faith. As you grow in your faith, obstacles will be overcome and hinderances removed, such that you will be free to "keep all things" that Jesus has commanded. This exercise must then become part of your daily routine, precisely because you believe.

[181] Isaiah 18:4
[182] John 16:33

Talk to God about your struggles. Seek His presence to renew your strength and confidence.[183] If possible, remove yourself from your current situation. With courage, decide and take a stance or position consistent with the eternal vision of the Kingdom. Ask yourself if there is anything within your power and responsibility that you can do.[184] Remove the physical or mental obstacles that are causing you to stumble or become discouraged. Fight for your holiness.[185] Stop the meaningless talk, justifications, and speculations. *Be* the person of faith that God wants you to be.

Knowing God's "very great and precious promises," the apostle Peter urges us to strive "to add to our faith goodness; and to kindness, knowledge; and to knowledge, self-control; and to self-control, perseverance; and to perseverance, godliness; and to godliness, mutual affection; and to mutual affection, love". With these qualities growing and active in our lives, we will not be ineffective and unproductive.[186] Our desert crossing will not be easy, but it has its reward. Through our faith in Christ, we rely on the presence and intimacy of God,[187] which will ultimately be revealed on the other side, when we finally enter the Promised Land:

---

[183] Hebrews 12:12; 2 Peter 4:11

[184] Hebrews 12:12-13

[185] Hebrews 12:14

[186] 2 Peter 1:3-9

[187] Deuteronomy 31:6; Matthew. 28:20; 1 Timothy 6:12; Hebrews 4:11

> Now if we are children, then we are heirs—heirs of God and co-heirs with Christ, if indeed we share in his sufferings in order that we may also share in his glory. Romans 8:17

> "Look! God's dwelling place is now among the people, and he will dwell with them. They will be his people, and God himself will be with them and be their God. Revelation 21:3

Nearing the end of his words and instructions to the new generation of Israelites, Moses offers the people some final advice before they finally enter the Promised Land. He then appoints Joshua as their new leader and sings a final song of worship to the Lord, thanking Him for His faithfulness to the people all these years. Finally, Moses climbs Mount Nebo, where he would see the Promised Land from afar, before being collected by God in his death. Now, *Between Fear and Faith*, the new generation had to make their choice:

> See, I set before you today life and prosperity, death and destruction. For I command you today to love the Lord your God, to walk in obedience to him, and to keep his commands, decrees and laws; then you will live and increase, and the Lord your God will bless you in the land you are entering to possess. But if your heart turns away and you are not obedient, and if you are drawn away to bow down to other gods and worship them, I declare to you this day that you will certainly be destroyed. You will not live long in the

land you are crossing the Jordan to enter and possess.[188]

Clearly, God wanted this new plan to work. Despite the first attempt failing, the Lord offered the blessings of the new land once again in hopes that the people would reciprocate this opportunity with their love. Indeed, His commandment had been (and still is) an invitation to love. God invites us to love. He wants us to love Him with all our hearts and all that we are. It is a commandment, but it is also an invitation.

Faced with such a responsibility, it is natural to observe the seriousness with which Moses addressed the people. He knew much was at stake. His appeal is dramatic and emphatic, as he was aware this would be the people's last chance to place their fear in the Lord:

> This day I call the heavens and the earth as witnesses against you that I have set before you life and death, blessings, and curses. Now *choose life*, so that you and your children may live and that you may love the Lord your God, listen to his voice, and hold fast to him. For the Lord is your life, and he will give you many years in the land he swore to give to your fathers, Abraham, Isaac and Jacob.[189]

Moses was concerned that the people of Israel would forget God. They would certainly prosper in Canaan, and

---

[188] Deuteronomy 30:15-18
[189] Deuteronomy 30:19-20

that could eventually become a distraction in their love for the Lord. George Bernard Shaw puts it in a simple yet powerful fashion: "There are two tragedies in life. One is not to get your heart's desire. The other is to get it."[190] The forty years of torturous waiting was about to end, and Moses needed to make sure they ended well.

Between fear and faith, choose faith, and faith in God!

I cannot imagine what was going through Moses' mind when he learned that, after eighty years of wandering in the desert since he fled Egypt, he would be forbidden by God to enter the Promised Land. Perhaps this final achievement had become an obsession for the old leader. He had been the central figure in the entire process and all its intricacies. He delivered the people from Pharaoh in Egypt and carefully guided them through the desert, turning what had simply been a dream of freedom into reality. Humanly speaking, if there was a giant in this story, it would have to be Moses. And despite all this, he would not be permitted to enter the Promised Land. Moses was

---

[190]George Bernard Shaw, Man and Superman: A Comedy and a Philosophy, Archibald Constable, Westminster, 1903, Act IV, Quote Page 174

taken by the Lord to Mount Nebo, where he was only allowed to behold the land from afar, just before passing.

I confess I always had a feeling of frustration regarding this episode in Moses' life. After years of service and a highly unique friendship with God, one where "the LORD would speak to Moses face to face, as one speaks to a friend,"[191] he would not be responsible for the final chapters of this narrative. Though the Lord had not forgotten him, and it is true He left for a place eternally better than Canaan; it would still have been a triumphant ending to know that Moses, along with Caleb and Joshua, had crossed the Jordan River together.

However, that was not so—it was so much better. By gaining heaven, that patient and humble man, one who had been "more humble than anyone else on the face of the earth,"[192] had gained Canaan as well. It's always like that, you know? How the bigger dreams always get the smaller ones thrown in? About 1,400 years after his own death, Moses finally got that dream fulfilled. Remember that time when Jesus took Peter, James, and John up the mountain with Him to pray? His face was changed, and His clothes became white, dazzling like lightening. And there, by His side, stood Moses, along with Elijah.[193]

---

[191] Exodus 33:11

[192] Numbers 12:3

[193] The account of Jesus' transfiguration in Matthew 17; Luke 9.

Finally, after so long, there he was: on a mountaintop, right in the middle of the Promised Land.

Indeed, God does not forget those who love Him.

9 781738 045600